# Locations of Front Cover Photos

① Wigwam Motel, AZ

② Lighthouse B & B, MN

③ Manresa Castle, WA

④ Treebones Resort, CA

⑤ Moose Meadow Lodge Treehouse, VT

⑥ 1926 C & O Caboose, VA

⑦ Spruce Mountain Lookout, WY

⑧ Abbey Road Farm, OR

⑨ Dr. Clark Park Inn, ID

# Location of Back Cover Photo

⑩ The Shire of Montana, MT

# Quirky Sleeps

Some of America's Most Fun Places to Spend the Night

Bruce & Susan Armstrong

# Quirky Sleeps
## Some of America's Most Fun Places to Spend the Night

ISBN: 978-0-692-24261-2

Published by:
Armstrong Travel Ventures, LLC
1380 Marlin Drive
Naples, FL 34102
www.ArmstrongTravelVentures.com

This book was printed in the United States of America.

# Table of Contents

## Quirky Sleeps by State

# California

# Colorado

# Connecticut

# Florida

# Georgia

## Minnesota

## Mississippi

## Missouri

## Montana

## Nebraska

## New Hampshire

## New Jersey

## New Mexico

## New York

## North Carolina

## Ohio

## Oregon

## Pennsylvania

## Rhode Island

## South Carolina

## Wisconsin

## Wyoming

# Quirky Sleeps by Genre

## Boats

## Cabooses and Other Railroad Cars

## Castles

## Caves

## Jails

## Lighthouses

## Schools

## Tepees, Tents and Yurts

## Themed Rooms

## Travel Trailers

## Tree Houses

## Wigwams

## Wildlife Lookout Towers

## Wildlife Refuges

## Everything Else — The Eclectics

# Introduction

Are you ready to have some fun on your next road trip? Adventure awaits you, if you choose to give it a go. What do you need to do to experience the adventure? Simply choose to spend the night someplace quirky — like a tree house, or a castle, or a caboose — instead of in one of America's ubiquitous travel motels that stack up at Interstate highway exits. Those motels may be what you need, when a place to sleep is all you need, but few people would call them interesting, unusual or fun.

To be quirky a place needs character, a peculiar trait, an idiosyncrasy; it must have an individualizing quality. People will have different views of what is quirky. If you live in a tree house, staying in a tree house may not be quirky to you, but it will be an unusual experience for most people. We spent several years compiling a list of publicly available lodging in railroad cars, tepees, castles, caves, Hobbit homes, jails and other places that looked to be quirky and fun. Then we decided it was time for us to hit the road in order to, literally, check into these places.

We drove around the lower 48 states for over 100 days staying at as many of these quirky sleeps as we could, and visiting many others for a first hand evaluation. Some places on our initial list fell off — closed, not quite as they were advertised to be, or not readily available to the general public. We added more places to our list as people volunteered suggestions, once they learned of our quest. We are sure to have missed some worthy places along the way, but we did find a lot of them. When we returned home, our car had over 22,000 more miles on it than when we left, and we had checked out nearly 150 places.

Our extensive road trip was an amazing experience. The vast majority of the places we stayed at exceeded our expectations for comfort, camaraderie and fun. These places are often the manifestation of their creators' passion. As much as the places, the people made the trip extraordinary. The owners of these quirky sleeps often have fascinating stories, and our fellow guests were usually interesting adventurers as well.

In fact, one of the delightful differences of staying at a quirky sleep is the social aspect. At a travel motel, you may have a pleasant conversation with the check-in clerk, and may exchange a few words with fellow guests on the elevator or at breakfast, but that is normally the extent of any socializing. At a quirky sleep, you usually will meet the owners. If you show any interest in their place, you may hear their story and be given a peek behind the scenes. Many places introduce their guests to each other, offer afternoon teas or cocktail hours, or have gathering places like hot tubs or fire pits. We met some wonderful owners and guests on our trip.

Staying at all these quirky places made our road trip one of the most fun and interesting trips we have taken. We fully expect to return to many of them because we enjoyed them so much. We encourage you to get out there and give some of these places a try. We think you'll like the experience. And if you run across any quirky sleeps we didn't include in this book, please let us know. We may be able to include them at a later time.

We wish you safe, adventurous, and fun travels.

Bruce and Susan

# How to Use This Book

Quirky sleeps, by definition, have some individualizing quality, but many can be classified into genres, as well. A number of quirky sleeps are cabooses, or castles, or tree houses, for example. So we include a short explanation of the quirky sleep genres we cover. For readers who are interested in a particular type of quirky sleep, there is a list by genre in the Table of Contents. Places that have more than one type of lodging may appear several times.

The book is organized by state, and within the state, its quirky sleeps are in alphabetical order. A map at the beginning of each write-up shows the location of that lodging within the state. This geographical presentation should be the most useful to travelers.

Within each place write-up, we describe the experience of staying there. We tell you if the experience is rustic, and the degree of rusticity. We comment if water or electric is absent. We let you know if there is, or isn't, a bathroom en suite, whether the bathroom has modern fixtures, or is an outhouse (very few), or is shared.

We tell you of the few places where you need to bring linens, a sleeping bag, a pillowcase or towels. We tell you if any meals are provided, as many of these quirky sleeps are bed and breakfasts, several provide dinner, and some places you need to provide a meal or two yourself.

We point out any things we thought were particularly noteworthy, like being child friendly, having incredible scenery, or being spectacularly romantic. We let you know if there is air conditioning, or heating. We give you an indication of cost using a range of dollar signs:

| | |
|---|---|
| $ | < $100 |
| $$ | $100 - $150 |
| $$$ | $150 - $200 |
| $$$$ | $200 - $250 |
| $$$$$ | > $250 |

These costs are meant to give you an indication of prices for one night, double-occupancy, but you need to read the fine print. Sometimes a two-night or longer stay is required. Sometimes the price includes up to three meals with complimentary wine. Sometimes package deals are available. Use the $$$'s as a guideline only.

What we have not done is provide an overall rating, like one-star or three-stars. These quirky sleeps represent a wide range of experiences. One of the most rustic experiences, for instance, requires a canoe trip of several hours to reach a tree house with no electric or water, requires using an outhouse, and requires providing your own meals. We thought it was a great adventure and loved it, but recognize some readers would not. So instead of giving it a four-star rating, we describe it and let you decide how well you might like it.

We provide the name, address, telephone numbers and website of each place to enable you to contact them. We have endeavored to ensure accuracy, but sometimes phone numbers and websites change. If our information doesn't connect you, you will probably have enough information to make a successful Internet search to find them.

We have attempted to be comprehensive, accurate and fair in our comments. We have described these quirky places as we found them in the summer of 2013. You should contact them before visiting, as things change. We know that several of these places were in the process of adding additional lodging when we were there. Any errors or omissions in our comments are solely our responsibility.

# Quirky Sleeps Travel Tips

Quirky sleeps are different from standard travel motels, and different from each other, so we found carrying a few extra items enhanced our ability to enjoy our experiences.

Carry a small, soft-sided overnight bag with you. One that is big enough to hold two days of clothing and your toiletries should do fine. Many of the quirky sleeps have steps or entrances that would make lugging a large suitcase into them difficult (like a tree house, or caboose). We each travelled with a large suitcase in our car, but loaded two days of clothing at a time into the small bags, and that worked well. At times, we used backpacks when we were doing something that made it prudent to have both hands free (like getting into and out of boats at lighthouses).

Carry two night-lights, one that plugs into house electric and one that operates on a battery. Quirky sleeps come in different shapes, sometimes with unusual obstructions on your path to the bathroom. We found our nightlights helpful for orienting ourselves when awakening in unfamiliar surroundings.

Carry a small flashlight in your overnight bag. Some quirky sleeps require a short walk outside to the restroom. Purchasing a headlamp is even better. A headlamp leaves both hands free for whatever you are doing. They are available at stores selling camping supplies.

Bring along a cooler. Many quirky sleeps are B & B's, but some aren't. Most are near restaurants, but not all. Several times we stopped at a store, bought the makings for dinner or breakfast, and put them in the cooler along with some ice. When we didn't need the cooler for food, we stored other items in it. If you happen to visit quirky sleeps in wine country, your cooler will protect any wine you purchase from excessive summer heat in a parked vehicle.

Only a handful of our quirky sleeps were so isolated that we had to prepare our own breakfast or dinner, but several of our all-time favorites are among them. We recommend carrying instant coffee, salt & pepper, a small container of cooking oil, and a handful of restaurant packets of mustard, mayo and ketchup. A box of breakfast cereal can come in handy. A roll of heavy-duty aluminum foil makes cooking many things on a grill possible. Pack some matches. Bring a roll of paper towels along. Every place we stayed where we needed to cook provided basic cooking utensils and dishes, but we recommend packing a set of silverware per person, plus tongs for moving food on a grill.

Regardless of what you pack, when you make a reservation at a quirky sleep where you will be cooking, ask them what cooking utensils and dishes are supplied. Also ask about cooking basics like butter, oil, coffee, milk, etc. That way there will be no surprises.

Bring along binoculars. Some of our quirky sleeps are located amidst awesome scenery, with good wildlife viewing available, as well.

Carry disposable earplugs in your toiletries. They will not stop you from hearing anything you really need to hear, like a fire alarm, but they will mute unfamiliar noises that can ruin your sleep. These can include noisy window air-conditioners, loud animal noises like tree frogs if you're in a canvas cabin, nearby highway noise, or even a foghorn at a lighthouse.

# Quirky Sleep Genres

## Boats

Being near water has a tranquil effect on almost everybody. Maybe that is why 40% of the US population lives on the 10% of land that borders an ocean, and why so many people vacation on beaches, lakes and streams. Sleeping on a boat is the nearest you can be to water while still staying dry.

The most common experience of sleeping on a boat today is being on a cruise ship. But cruise ships are not quirky and we don't cover them here. Spending the night on tall ships, small yachts or an historic passenger ship is quirky, and there are several places you can do that. The tall ships conjure thoughts of exploration and exciting ports. You can feel the gentle rock of the ship, and hear wind in the rigging and the soft creaking of mast timbers as you drift off to sleep in a snug cabin.

Being aboard an historic passenger ship puts you back in a bygone era of luxury sailing. Small yachts let you hear the lap of gentle waves lulling you to sleep. And is there any better image of someone who has it made than someone who owns a yacht? Well you, too, can own a yacht, even if it's only for a day!

## Cabooses and Railroad Cars

The origin of the iconic caboose railroad car dates back to the 1840's when Conductor Nat Williams of the Auburn & Syracuse line set up shop at the end of a train on an old boxcar. Soon other conductors commandeered railcars and followed suit. Some used boxcars, and others built a shanty on a flatcar for their office.

The most common style of caboose in the United States has a cupola in the roofline. This innovation is credited to Conductor T. B. Watson of the Chicago and North West Railway. In 1863, he set up shop in a boxcar that had a hole in the roof. He found that riding with his head above the car gave him a better ability to monitor the train, so he glassed it in.

Railroads began manufacturing cabooses with cupolas specifically designed for conductors' use after that. In the eastern United States, the cupolas were usually in the center of the car. Out west, the railroads preferred the cupola offset to one end of the car.

In 1923, the Akron, Canton and Youngstown Railroad eliminated the cupola and installed bay windows on both sides of the car. This design improved visibility and eliminated some height problems in old tunnels. Bay windows became a standard design industry-wide.

Cabooses were required on trains in the United States until the 1980's. By that time remote monitoring of the trains became reliable enough that railroads could save money by retiring these non-revenue producing cars, and the men who rode them.

Today, cabooses are re-purposed for many uses, including lodging. In fact, we have more listings for cabooses than any other category of quirky sleep. The variations in caboose design, such as having a cupola or a bay window and its location in the car, fosters creativity while turning a caboose into a lodging. We stayed in quite a few cabooses and never saw two that were exactly the same.

In addition to cabooses, we also include a smattering of other railcars — boxcars, passenger cars, and even one diesel locomotive.

## Castles

Europe has authentic castles — built hundreds of years ago by royalty, sprouting towers and parapets, surrounded by moats, perhaps hiding dungeons. Medieval villages sprang up around them and the castles served as defensive fortresses to ward off attacks.

There are no authentic American castles in that sense, but there are a number of large edifices, mostly built between 1880 and 1910, that were built to emulate castles. Some do that quite well. Some were built to resemble ancestral homes and others were based on favorite castles. Several incorporate windows and woodwork taken from real castles. Knights may never have jousted on the grounds, but they are quirky and fun places to stay.

## Caves

There are not many places where you can sleep in a cave, but we found a few. Sleeping in them is a unique experience. They are very quiet and no heating or air-conditioning is necessary because they stay at a near constant temperature year round. Natural caves have fascinating formations inside them to contemplate.

If you are thinking that sleeping in a cave is going to take you back 100,000 years to a rock bed and open fire in the floor, not so. The caves listed here are pretty plush. And you are not allowed to do any drawing on the cave walls.

## Jails

Perhaps we need to be more specific — former jails. And you do not have to sleep on a thin mattress in a bunk, eat prison rations or restrict your movements. All our listed jails are comfortable B & B's. They do have quirky histories and some of the rooms may have old cell components or memorabilia around. All of them were active for many years and have some tales of notorious prisoners and prison escapes to tell. If you spend the night, you can count on making bail the next morning, right after breakfast.

## Lighthouses

Lighthouses were constructed to serve one of two critical functions. They either warned mariners of a particular danger, or they beckoned mariners through a safe passage. They did so by sending out a signal light that was unique in its length or pulse, so that mariners could precisely locate their position.

Today, lighthouses are an anachronism in the age of Global Positioning Systems. Many lighthouses have been shut down, and those that do remain active have been automated. The US government has sold many of them, or their keeper's quarters, to groups or individuals who wish to preserve them. And many of these have become B & B's in order to generate the funds needed to maintain them.

Staying at a lighthouse has a particular charm. You are guaranteed a nice, waterfront view. Generally you will either have a chance to see a spectacular sunrise or sunset. And there is something nostalgic about experiencing this aspect of our maritime history.

## Schools

Ever want to fall asleep in class? Well, now you can and not worry about getting into any trouble. An eclectic collection of former school buildings has been turned into quirky lodging. The schools vary from historic, one-room schoolhouses up to pretty large elementary schools and can be anything from basic lodging, to B & B's to hotels. Many have old photographs of the schools when they were active and lots of memorabilia that may remind you of your own school days.

## Tepees, Tents and Yurts

All the places in this broad category have two things in common: they all consist of some type of canvas abode and they represent quintessential travel lodging. The tepee was the lodging of our Native-American plains Indians who needed shelters that could be moved seasonally to follow the bison. The yurt, with its circular shape and peaked roof, served the same purpose for the nomadic tribes of Mongolia. And the tent is how Americans began to travel after the automobile became widespread, but before the advent of the motel industry.

Only one of the lodgings in this category has you sleeping on the ground in a sleeping bag. All the others put you in a comfortable bed with a permanent floor under you. The places range from basic canvas cabins to yurts that are air-conditioned and have an en suite bath and shower. They can be quite commodious.

## Themed Rooms

We include two types of quirky places in this category. We cover several places that devote the entire facility to an era, like the 1940's, or the 1950's. The décor, the music that is playing, the DVD's available in the rooms, are all designed to take you back to another time.

We also cover several places where the individual rooms are designed to a theme. The themes range from children's fantasies, to nostalgia, to adventures, to romance, and to the bawdy. If you ever wanted to be an Egyptian Queen, a pirate, an astronaut, or a Gypsy for a day, these places can provide the right environment for your fantasy.

## Travel Trailers

If you ever wondered what was inside those stainless-steel Airstream trailers you've seen on the road, here's your chance to find out. If you've ever wondered what people taking road trips in 1950's and 1960's vintage trailers were experiencing, here's your chance. We include several places that have restored Airstreams and vintage travel trailers to stay in. You can indulge a little curiosity and stay in one of them yourself.

## Tree houses

A tree house has an innate appeal to the child in us, that child who once climbed trees just for fun. Some of us built tree forts or clubhouses in our youth ("No Girls Allowed"). We imagined living the adventure of the Swiss Family Robinson, surviving on a tropical island in a massive tree house. We cover a number of places that will let you sleep in the forest canopy, and girls are definitely allowed.

These tree houses come in shades of authenticity. A true tree house would be built in the trees with no support other than the trees. We cover those, but also include tree houses built in the trees, but on ground supports, and even a quirky house among the trees. All our tree houses give you the feel of being in the trees, regardless of construction. Try them — unleash your inner squirrel!

## Wigwams

The wigwams we include look like Native-American tepees, but rather than being made of canvas, they are permanent buildings with wood or steel frames, cement walls and adobe finishes. As permanent buildings, they have baths, showers, air-conditioning, electric, heat, lockable doors — all the aspects of a motel room, but they have a round base and conical walls that slant in toward the top of the tepee. They are named incorrectly, as wigwams were more permanent huts used by eastern Native-Americans, not the mobile tepees of the nomadic plains Indians, but don't let that get in the way of the fun.

These wigwam villages are quirky throwbacks to the early days of the motor travel lodging industry in the 1930's, 1940's and 1950's. Most inland vacation travel in the early 1900's was by train. By the 1920's, the automobile was the preferred method of travel, and camping by the car was the normal overnight lodging. In the 1930's, problems with common latrines and showers at the campgrounds led to the beginning of the motel industry, typically in small individual cabins, sometimes whimsically done.

In 1933, Frank Redford of Kentucky built a tepee-shaped building to house his collection of Native-American artifacts as both a museum and shop. The following year he built a few more such structures on the property to encourage visitors to spend the night. In 1936, he was granted a patent for his Wigwam Motel concept.

From 1933 to 1949, seven Wigwam Villages were built across the country. Today, three survive: one in Arizona along historic Route 66 (#6), one in California, also along Route 66 (#7), and one near Cave City, Kentucky (#2). There is a similar facility in Texas that was not part of Redford's chain. Kids love to stay at them.

## Wildfire Lookout Towers

Wildfire lookout towers were the front line in forest fire spotting before the advent of satellites. Some still play a role in wildfire monitoring, but many are no longer manned. A few of these towers have been made available for guest lodging. They are difficult to get into because they are so popular. If you stay in one, you are guaranteed a spectacular view of some awesome scenery.

## Wildlife Refuges

We cover three wildlife refuges that offer the opportunity to stay on the premises after the gates have closed to the day visitors. One houses domestic wildlife, such as bison, elk, bear and bobcats. One houses rescued big cats, such as tigers, lions, and panthers. One houses African and Asian animals, such as rhino, antelope and wild horses. All of them are fascinating places to spend the night.

## Everything Else — The Eclectics

We cover many unique places, one-of-a-kind or two-of-a-kind types of quirky sleeps. Some of our favorite places fall in this un-categorized category. They include grain silos, slave quarters, Hobbit homes, an underwater lodge, a bank, a dog-shaped house, sharecroppers' shacks and more. These places exhibit some of the most creative and interesting lodging in the book.

# A Few of Our Favorite Things
## (In no particular order)

The baked eggs, and the fresh peaches with basil and cream, at the Cherry Wood Bed, Breakfast and Barn, Washington

Driving a 100-year-old Model T Ford at the Tin Lizzie Inn, California

The luxurious beds and sheets at Ravenwood Castle, Ohio

Steaming sunrise coffee on the deck of the Tall Ship Manitou, Michigan

The funky cellblock room at the Jailhouse Inn Bed & Breakfast, Minnesota

Being surrounded by hummingbirds, and the breathtaking morning view, at the Kokopelli Cave, New Mexico

The restored antiques and western ambience at The Wyman Hotel, Colorado

The best scones we've ever had at the Jailhouse Inn Bed & Breakfast, Minnesota

The sumptuous railcar suite at the Whistle Stop B & B, Minnesota

The cave bathroom at the Old Jail Bed & Breakfast, Minnesota

The canoe trip to and from the Edisto River Treehouses, South Carolina

The Doo Wop music at The Caribbean Motel, New Jersey

The gourmet dinner at The Norumbega Inn, Maine

The portraits, antique cars and sunsets at the Keeper's House Inn, Maine

Free popcorn and the fire pit at Adventure Suites, New Hampshire

The history, from Ethan Allen to hippie communes, surrounding Guilford Schoolhouse #10, Vermont

The children-friendly atmosphere of the Red Caboose Motel and Restaurant, Pennsylvania

The outstanding Treebear Porridge at the LaVoie Treehouse, Minnesota

The wildlife tour and luxury yurt at Nomad Ridge at The Wilds, Ohio

The seclusion, and the outdoors shower, at Middle Island Lighthouse, Michigan

The renovation story of Sand Hill Lighthouse, Michigan

The communal breakfast featuring oatmeal with homemade granola at A Teton Treehouse, Wyoming

The fanciful lights of the Shire of Montana at night, Montana

The Observatory and Rainbow Bridge at the Cedar Creek Treehouse, Oregon

The Toasty Toes Turndown Service at Lakedale Resort at Three Lakes, Washington

The relaxing soaking pool at McMenamin's Kennedy School, Oregon

The elegantly served, four-course breakfast in the Dining Car of the Red Caboose Getaway Inn, Washington

The ubiquitous music, the walking tour, the organic breakfast and the overall ambiance at Abbey Road Farms B & B, Oregon

The dramatic cliffside setting of the Haceta Head Light Station, Oregon

The total experience of staying at the East Brother Light Station, California

The night sky view from Mt. Palomar at Camp Ribbonwood, California

The superb theme executions at The Victorian Mansion, California

5 o'clock cocktails and the relaxed atmosphere at the Palm Springs Rendezvous, California

The impromptu cocktail circle at The Blue Swallow Inn, New Mexico

The healing massage at the Rainbow Hearth Sanctuary, Texas

The music, atmosphere and history at The Shack Up Inn, Mississippi

Living off the grid at the Heliohouse Earthship, New Mexico

The historic authenticity of the Thornewood Castle, Washington

The heart-shaped Jacuzzi tub in the trees at The Original Treehouse Cottages, Arkansas

# Alaska Wilderness Guides

16001 Carl Street
Anchorage, AK 99516
907-345-4470
www.akwild.com
Eric Schmidt, Owner
$$$$$

Once each summer, Eric Schmidt offers two guests what he calls the "Five Day Treehouse Stay", a guided tree house stay in the Alaskan wilderness. You fly from Anchorage in a floatplane that lands on a remote, ridge-top lake. From there you hike two miles to your destination, where you take up residence in the comfortable tree house that Eric used while building his cabin. He takes up residence in the cabin.

For the next three days, you can hike, fish or just view the wildlife. Eric is available to provide suggestions and to guide you in whatever activities you choose. Eric also provides all your meals during your stay.

On the fifth morning, you will raft five miles to another lake, because the lake you landed on is not large enough for a loaded plane to take off. When you reach that lake, you will help hoist the raft you used into a tree. It will be retrieved by snow machine during the winter and returned to the tree house. You will then be flown back to Anchorage.

Alaska Wilderness Guides has been in business since 1977 and has been owned by Eric since 1992. Eric is trained in both Arctic Survival and Wilderness Emergency Medicine. The price for this five-day, four night excursion includes your flights to and from the tree house, lodging, all meals and guide services.

We are including this very unique tree house adventure in the book, but our own quirky sleep travels have, so far, been confined to the lower 48 states. Therefore, we have not personally had the opportunity to experience this trip.

# Aurora Express Bed & Breakfast

P. O. Box 80128
Fairbanks, AK 99708
800-221-0073   907-474-0949
www.aurora-express.com
Mike and Susan Wilson, Owners
$$ - $$$

The Aurora Express is the creation of Mike and Susan Wilson, who at one time worked together helping to build the Trans Alaskan Pipeline. They purchased three former Alaska Railroad cars from the Denali Hotel, moved the cars to Fairbanks, put them onto 700 feet of track on 16 acres of land overlooking the Tanana River and Fairbanks, and renovated them into a unique Alaskan B & B. They have since added a caboose and dining car to their collection.

The Aurora Express lodging cars are:

*"National Domain"* – this adults-only car has been renovated into four suites. Each suite has a queen bed, private bath and entrance. The suites are individually decorated with Victorian themes and have 10-foot curved ceilings.

*"National Emblem"* – this children-friendly car has been renovated to its original state. It is a good choice for families and for people travelling in a group.

*"The Golden Nellie"* – this adults-only car was originally known as "Caboose #1068". It has been renovated to the height of luxury with golden ceilings, heavy burgundy velvet drapes and ornate furnishings.

*"Arlene"* – this car was originally used as a hospital car during WWII. It has been renovated into an 85-foot long private car with two bedrooms, one bath and a living room with TV.

In addition to the lodging cars, *"The Diner Car"* seats 24 for breakfast, which is served each day at 8:00, and is sometimes accompanied by entertainment.

The Aurora Express is open from May 25 until September 5 each year.

As previously mentioned, our quirky sleep travels have, so far, been confined to the lower 48 states. Therefore, we have not personally had the opportunity to experience staying here.

# The Canyon Motel & RV Park

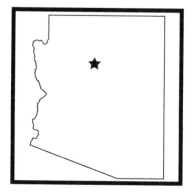

1900 East Rodeo Road (Historic Route 66)
Williams, AZ 86046
800-482-3955   928-635-9371
www.thecanyonmotel.com
$$

Williams, Arizona is located on I-40, just 50 miles south of the Grand Canyon. The Canyon Motel offers you the opportunity to spend your night in an historic railcar before driving, or riding the nostalgic Grand Canyon Railroad, up to Grand Canyon Village.

The Canyon Motel has three railcars for lodging. They have two offset cupola cabooses, one of which is said to be haunted. Both cabooses are painted red and spent their working life on the Atchison, Topeka & Santa Fe Railroad. They also have a Pullman car from the Grand Canyon Railroad that has been remodeled into three private rooms with private entrances.

We stayed in one of the Pullman car rooms. It was spacious and housed a queen bed, full couch, flat-screen TV, a small fridge and microwave, built in desk and separate bath and shower. The curved ceiling was wood and the walls were nicely painted in desert tones. The lights were old railroad lanterns turned into wall lamps and there were several old railroad pictures and posters on the walls.

In addition to the rail cars, the Canyon Motel also has 18 cottage rooms styled from the 1940's. They are located in six flagstone buildings, and were the original lodging available at the motel before the rail cars were added. The property also includes an RV park and several of the RV's are available for rent.

Guests at the Canyon Motel have access to their pool, outdoor grills and a playground and laundry facility. The staff is friendly, and the Canyon Motel is child-friendly with its playground and pool. There are hummingbird feeders near the office and just watching the hummingbirds is entertaining.

The Canyon Motel is open year-round.

# Grand Canyon Caverns Suite

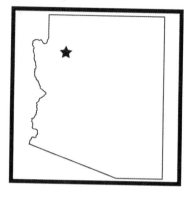

Mile 115, Route 66
Peach Springs, AZ 86434
928-422-3223
www.gccaverns.com
$$$$$

Grand Canyon Caverns Suite offers the opportunity for up to six people to sleep in a 65 million year old cave, 220 feet underground. The cavern is so far underground that there is not only no natural light — absolutely nothing lives there except you.

The cavern is huge. It measures 200 feet by 400 feet and the roof is 70 feet tall. It is the largest dry cavern in the United States. It is furnished with two double beds. There is a queen-size foldout sofa in the living room area, as well as an historic book and magazine collection to browse through.

The cavern is open to tours throughout the day, so overnight guests go in with the last tour and check out before the first tour the next day. Someone is on duty 24 hours a day above, should you need to contact anyone during your stay.

Wigwam Village #7, CA

Turpentine Creek Wildlife Refuge, AR

# Noftsger Hill Inn

425 E. North Street
Globe, AZ 85501
928-425-2260
www.noftsgerhillinn.com
Rosalie & Dom Ayala, Owners
$ - $$

The Noftsger Hill Inn sits atop a hill overlooking the Cobre Valley and the historic mining town of Globe, Arizona, home of the Old Dominion Mine. Gold, silver and copper were discovered nearby in the late 1800's and miners flocked to the area.

In 1907, the North Globe Schoolhouse opened on Noftsger Hill, which was named after a prominent settler who sold water to the mines. In 1917, an addition was added to the front, bringing the building to its present footprint. The expanded building was known as the Noftsger Hill School. The school was active from 1907 through 1981 educating Arizonans, including former Governor Rose Mofford.

Our bedroom at the Noftsger Hill Inn was the largest room we have ever slept in. It was an entire, large classroom, which still had its original hardwood floors and the classroom blackboard (with chalk). The room was furnished with a king bed, couch and coffee table, fireplace, TV, antiques and area rugs. A private bath occupied the former coatroom and had a claw-foot tub and shower. Other rooms were furnished similarly, but with southwest, Spanish and Victorian themes.

The large main hallway, which was the old assembly area, held several seating areas with reading materials and area memorabilia. Antiques lined the walls, including some old reading exercises on easels and many class photos.

Breakfast was served in the former kindergarten classroom located off the main hallway. It consisted of juice, fruit with yogurt and granola, a garden quiche (from Rosalie's garden), toast, and very good coffee.

The Noftsger Hill Inn is open year round.

# The Phantom Ranch

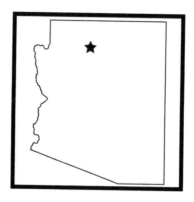

Grand Canyon National Park, AZ
928-638-2631
reserve-gcsr@xanterra.com
$

The Phantom Ranch is located at the bottom of the Grand Canyon on the north side of the Colorado River and along Bright Angel Creek. The property consists of rustic cabins built in 1922 out of native wood and stone.

There are three ways to get to the Phantom Ranch. You can hike in and out on the Bright Angel or South Kiabob Trails, you can ride mules down and up the South Kiabob Trail, or you can raft in and either hike or ride a mule out. We rafted in and hiked out on the Bright Angel Trail for our stay.

The accommodations at the ranch are either dormitories or cabins. There are two dormitories, one each for men and women. The dorms each have ten bunk beds, a shower and a restroom. There are eleven cabins. Most are equipped with four bunk beds, a cold-water sink, and toilet. Showers are located in a central location. All accommodations include soap and towels.

A canteen building serves meals, beverages and sells sundries. We arrived in the afternoon and had a hearty stew for dinner. After dinner the canteen closed for cleanup, then re-opened as a pub serving beer for a few hours. Since we were hiking out, we chose their early breakfast seating and took along a sack lunch for the hike.

The hike out is strenuous. The Bright Angel Trail is 9.9 miles long, measured from the Phantom Ranch, and rises 4,380 feet to the top. We kept up a pretty good pace and the climb took us six hours. You can arrange to have a duffel bag carried out by mule train, to lighten your load for the hike.

The Phantom Ranch takes reservations up to 13 months in advance, and is very popular. Be sure to reserve all your meals at the time you reserve lodging. Food and supplies can only get to the ranch by mule train. Summer temperatures at the bottom of the canyon can be very high.

# The Shady Dell

1 Douglas Road
Bisbee, AZ 85603
520-432-3567
www.theshadydell.com
Justin & Jen
$ - $$


The Shady Dell sits on a quiet lot on the east side of historic Bisbee, Arizona, just north of the Mexican border. The property traces its roots back to 1927, when it opened as a park providing camping spaces for travelers along US Highway 80, which ran from Savannah, Georgia to San Diego, California.

The Shady Dell no longer provides camping or RV spaces. What it does provide is a trip back to the 1950's by way of nine restored vintage trailers and one Chris Craft yacht. Each trailer accommodates two adults and is decorated to a 1950's theme. The vintage trailers are a 1957 El Rey, 1949 Airstream, 1950 Spartanette, 1951 Mansion, 1950 Manor, 1951 Royal Mansion, 1957 Airfloat, 1947 Tiki Bus (can sleep three), and a 1959 Boles Aero. You can also spend the night in the land-locked Chris Craft yacht.

Each of the trailers is equipped with a small fridge, a percolator and coffee, as well as linens and towels. A few trailers have a bath, but most trailers share a central bath and showers. The trailers have heating and swamp coolers. All trailers are non-smoking and there is a no-pet policy. No cooking facilities are in the trailers, and the 1950's style diner that is on the premises is there for looks only. Restaurants are nearby in Bisbee.

The Shady Dell closes for the coldest and warmest months in winter and summer. It is open from September through November and from March through May.

# Wigwam Motel

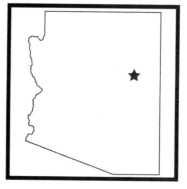

811 West Hopi Drive
Holbrook, AZ 86025
928-524-3048
www.sleepinginawigwam.com
$

In 1938, Chester E. Lewis saw the Wigwam Village in Cave City, Kentucky. Lewis owned a number of motels along Route 66, and in 1949 obtained a franchise to build a Wigwam Village in Holbrook, Arizona. His unique franchise arrangement was to put a coin operated radio in each wigwam. The radios played a half-hour of music for a dime and the dimes made up his franchise fee.

The Wigwam Motel is located on old Route 66 in Holbrook. It consists of 15 wigwams arranged on three sides of a square, with the office occupying the fourth side along the street. Each wigwam has a vintage car from the 1940's or 1950's permanently parked in front of it in the large, gravel lot. There are several other vintage cars parked around the office.

The wigwams are tepee-shaped structures that are made of wood frames and stucco. Each wigwam is equipped with a double bed, TV, heater, window air-conditioner, and one of the motel's original hickory chairs and tables. Each unit has a small bath and shower. In keeping with the 1950's theme, there are no telephones, Internet or ice machines. Wi-Fi is available in the office.

The motel operated from 1950 to 1974, when it closed after Interstate 40 caused traffic to bypass the town. It was renovated and re-opened in 1988 and is still run by the Lewis family. A small museum attached to the office displays some of Chester Lewis' collection of Native-American and petrified wood artifacts.

The motel is listed on the National Register of Historic Places, where it is officially known as Wigwam Village #6. The motel is open year round and children love the wigwams.

# Beckham Creek Cave Lodge

HC 72 Box 42
Parthenon, AR 72666
870-446-6043
www.beckhamcavelodge.com
$$$$$

The Beckham Creek Cave Lodge is located at the east end of the Spanish Piano Cave, four miles west of Parthenon, Arkansas. The cave extends over a mile and a half into the mountain, and is named for a huge, natural flagstone formation near its entrance.

In 1981, a wealthy individual purchased the cave and surrounding property and turned the first 6,000 square feet of the cave into a spacious, luxurious, bomb shelter home, convinced a nuclear war would happen soon. He dammed up the natural water flow to create a 750,000-gallon fresh water supply, and stored a three-year's supply of food inside.

The cave is a living cave and seeps water, making it expensive to maintain. It has passed through several owners and the current owners are operating it as very unique lodging. The cave has five bedrooms, a recreation room, a large great room with seating and dining areas facing the Spanish Piano formation, and a large, modern, well equipped kitchen. Each of the five bedrooms has a king bed and its own private bath. All the floors are granite tiled and the lighting shows off the spectacular natural formations of the cave.

The entrance to the cave has a large wooden deck, large parking area, stone outdoor grill and fire pit halfway up the side of the mountain and overlooking a stocked trout pond, Beckham Creek and a helipad for arriving guests. If you are coming by car instead of helicopter, the lodge is at the end of four miles of gravel road.

The entire cave rents to one party of two to ten guests at a time. You need to supply your own food, as it is some distance to any restaurants. Beckham Creek Cave Lodge is open year round.

# The Grand Treehouse Resort

350 W. Van Buren Street
Eureka Springs, AR 72632
479-253-8733
www.thetreehouses.com
$$ - $$$

The Grand Treehouse Resort invites guests to "sleep out on a limb" with them. The resort operates eight tree houses in Eureka Springs. The resort is on the trolley line, making it easy to get around town.

The tree houses are actually on stilts and located in the trees. They all have king or queen beds, a wet bar, a small fridge, microwave, coffee maker, toaster, dishes and utensils. There is a flat screen TV and a DVD player in each tree house and complimentary movies are available in the office.

All of the nicely appointed tree houses are heated and air-conditioned. There are gas fireplaces that are activated in the cooler weather. The rooms are equipped with a two-person Jacuzzi tub. The Grand Treehouse Resort is open year round.

View from Kokopelli Cave B & B, NM

Kokopelli Cave Bedroom

# Livingston Junction Cabooses and Depot

1 Stonehaven Lane
Eureka Springs, AR 72631
888-878-7246   479-253-7143
www.livingstonjunctioncabooses.com
$ - $$

Livingston Junction is located two miles north of Eureka Springs on Route 23. It operates three cabooses and a cabin built to resemble a train depot on wooded acreage overlooking Livingston Hollow and the junction of the rail spur to Eureka Springs. The Eureka Springs & Northwest Arkansas Railway excursion train, with its puffing, steam locomotive, comes past the property on its runs, adding even more of a railroad ambiance to your stay.

The cabooses and depot are each set in their own secluded space, providing privacy. Each has its own driveway, made to look like a railroad bed. And each has a large deck looking out to the hollow below and equipped with outdoor furniture, a hammock and a grill.

Caboose #101, built in 1967, is decorated in a country décor. It has a queen bed, private bath and shower. The kitchenette contains a sink, microwave, coffee maker, and refrigerator/freezer. An original brakeman's desk is located in the cupola and a hot tub is outside on the deck.

Caboose #102, built in 1930, has a curved roof and ceiling and is decorated in a Victorian style. It has a queen bed, private bath and shower. The kitchenette contains a sink, microwave, coffee maker, and refrigerator/freezer. This caboose does not have a hot tub.

Caboose #103, built in 1926, has an old west décor. It has a queen bed, private bath and shower. The kitchenette has a sink, microwave, coffee maker, and refrigerator/freezer. A hot tub is located on the outside deck.

The Junction Depot Cabin can sleep four people. It has a full kitchen, a dining area, and a living room with a fireplace and sofa bed. A queen bed is in the bedroom and both a Jacuzzi tub and shower are in the bath. This deck has the best view of the excursion train and has a hot tub.

Livingston Junction is meant for quiet relaxation, so there is no cable or Internet access. Livingston Junction is open year round.

# Oak Crest
## Cottages & Treehouses

526 West Van Buren (West Hwy 62)
Eureka Springs, AR 72632
479-253-9493
www.estreehouses.com
$$ - $$$

Oak Crest operates ten tree houses that are located about four miles from the office (address above) on a wooded property inside an automated gate. When you check in, you receive a garage door opener for the gate, along with the key to your tree house. The tree houses, in this case, are actually cottages on stilts in the trees, but their elevation and windows certainly give you a tree house experience.

Each tree house features a king bed, a Jacuzzi tub for two, a small fridge, microwave, small dining table, couch, fireplace, and flat screen TV. They are air-conditioned and have a modern bath with a shower. There is a back porch with a swing for two and a small table with two chairs. As a nice touch, we received a welcome note from owners Elaine and Don, and a basket of complimentary snacks.

Our tree house was named "Venice" and the pictures and decorations carried out that theme nicely. Another nice decorating touch was a tree trunk located in the center of the room with branches that were covered in small lights. It made it feel even more of a tree house during the day, and created a pleasant lighting effect in the evening.

While we were there, Oak Crest had three Hobbit Caves and three mini-castles under construction and they are now open. "Lord of the Rings" fans will recognize Hobbit Caves, abodes built into hillsides that emphasize creature comforts.

Eureka Springs is a tourist destination, so there are many restaurants nearby. Oak Crest is open year round.

# The Original Treehouse Cottages

165 West Van Buren (West Hwy 62)
Eureka Springs. AR 72632
479-253-8667
www.treehousecottages.com
Terry & Patsy Miller, Owners
$$$


The Original Treehouse Cottages consists of eight tree houses located in two nearby locations. The four original tree houses are located behind the office and gift shop in Eureka Springs proper. The four newer tree houses are located a quarter mile south of town on Hwy 23, nestled onto 33 acres of woods on a hillside. We stayed at the Bungalow Cottage in the new section.

Check-in for all of the tree house cottages is at the in-town address. We picked up our key there, and also picked out a complimentary DVD from their wide selection. Patsy Miller is a potter, and her pottery is on sale in the gift shop.

A tree house cottage is an apt description of the lodging, as the cottages are not suspended in the trees. They are built among the trees on posts, and are quite high up, at least 30 feet. The many floor-to-ceiling windows make the cottages airy, and give them an authentic tree house feel.

Our tree house featured beautiful wood floors and ceiling, a stone-face fireplace, a four-poster king bed, comfortable couch, and TV with satellite and DVD. The kitchen had a full refrigerator stocked with complimentary soda, along with orange juice and homemade pumpkin bread for our breakfast. The tree house had both a front and back porch with seating.

A heart-shaped Jacuzzi tub was perched in a small nook that extended from the back of the tree house and had windows on all three sides. When we relaxed in the tub, we felt that we were suspended in the trees.

Terry Miller built many of the wood features of the cottage, like the front door and the mantle over the fireplace, from the trees that were felled for the building of the cottage. Patsy Miller made all of the tiles in the kitchen and bath, as well as the dishes.

The Original Treehouse Cottages are open year round.

# Texaco Bungalow

77 Mountain Street
Eureka Springs, AR 72632
888-253-8093
www.texacobungalow.com
Melissa Greene, Hostess
$$

The Texaco Bungalow is a 1930's art deco style former service station that has been remodeled into two lodging units, a bungalow in the main building and a bungalette in the former garage. The two cottages have private entrances from a shared deck.

Each of the units is meant for two adults, no children and no pets. They are equipped with a full kitchen, comfortable seating and TV/VCR's. The bungalows are a short walking distance to the historic downtown with its shops, galleries, restaurants and nightlife.

We were unable to tour the bungalows because they were booked and occupied while we were there, but the property was well kept up and nicely decorated on the exterior. The Texaco Bungalow is open year round.

The Victorian Mansion, CA

Traverse Tall Ship Manitou, MI

# Turpentine Creek
# Wildlife Refuge

239 Turpentine Creek Lane
Eureka Springs, AR 72632
479-253-5841
www.turpentinecreek.org
$$ - $$$

In 1978, Don, Hilda and daughter Tanya Jackson rescued their first lion, a male named Bum. In 1992, the Jackson family was asked to rescue 38 lions and tigers being housed in three cattle trailers. In response, they founded the Turpentine Creek Wildlife Refuge on a 450-acre ranch located seven miles outside of Eureka Springs. The refuge rescues big cats from private owners who find that they cannot properly care for these large carnivores.

Today Turpentine Creek cares for over 115 big cats. The most prevalent species is tigers, but lions, panthers, bobcats and African servals also live there. In addition to the big cats, the refuge has also rescued a monkey, a coati, six black bear and a grizzly bear.

Lodging choices at Turpentine Creek include a tree house, two suites, and five Zulu safari tents. The tree house overlooks big cat habitats from its circular deck. The two suites are adjacent to a big cat habitat, as well.

We stayed in one of the Zulu safari tents. An octagonal wood deck connects the tents. The deck has a hot tub and a central fire pit available for guests. The tents are arranged to look out over the Arkansas landscape from a hilltop. Each tent has a deck with a table for four. The tents are air-conditioned and feature a full bath and shower, a flat screen TV, a gas fireplace, and small fridge. The canvas walls have at least $1,000 worth of artwork for sale decorating them.

Overnight guests receive a guided tour of the big cat habitats as part of their stay. After the refuge closes to day guests, overnight guests are invited to watch the staff feed the big cats. Guests can also wander the pathways between the habitats at their leisure. This is particularly fun because big cats are nocturnal and become more active as the sun goes down.

Turpentine Creek offers a great opportunity to stay in luxurious, quirky lodging, see the big cats in humane habitats, and go to sleep with the roar of lions in the background. And every dollar spent here on lodging, souvenirs or artwork helps the rescue mission. Turpentine Creek is open year round.

# Camp Ribbonwood

24635 Woodridge Lane
Oak Grove (Warner Springs), CA
619-818-9343
www.campribbonwood.com
Lane McClelland & Laurie Roberts, Owners
$$$

If you want to experience some magical stargazing, you need to stay at Camp Ribbonwood's luxurious safari tent. Named after the unique trees that grow there, Camp Ribbonwood is located about 20 miles southeast of Temecula on the northeast side of Mt Palomar. The lodging is tranquil, very private, close to nature, and has magnificent views over the valley to the north.

The safari tent is 16 by 20 stretched over cedar logs. It sits on the west end of an elevated 20 by 40 wooden deck, and half of the open deck has a canvas awning over it. The structure sits inside a fenced area and pets are welcome. Pets can be confined to the deck, or allowed to roam the enclosed property. A hot tub is located on the deck, along with two cushioned lounge chairs, a table and two chairs, and a charcoal kettle grill with a pizza oven attachment.

The tent is equipped with a queen bed, flat screen TV with DVD, two wooden rockers (made by Lane) facing a wood stove, a full kitchen with propane stove and oven, a microwave, small fridge and coffee maker, along with all the dishes and utensils you might need. The kitchen and bath walls are made of recycled pine. The modern bath has a sink, commode, claw-footed tub and shower.

There is no screening on the tent, and none is needed, as there are almost no insects in the dry climate. We saw a few moths flitting around our lights as we were reading at night, but that was it. We left the tent flaps open all night and enjoyed the cool evening air and the view of the stars from our pillows. With the flaps open, you can also relax with a soak in the claw-footed tub while you watch the sunset.

While there are restaurants in the area, once we were in this peaceful setting, we enjoyed grilling our dinner and enjoying the tranquility. If you stay here, do get up in the dark hours to gaze at the sky for a while. Camp Ribbonwood opened in May 2013 and is open year round.

# Costanoa

2001 Rossi Road at Hwy 1
Pescadero, CA 94060
877-262-7848   650-879-1100
www.costanoa.com
$ - $$

Costanoa is located on the east side of the Pacific Coast Highway just south of Pescadero, California. It offers the chance to stay in canvas bungalows within a large eco-friendly resort. In addition to the canvas bungalows, Costanoa has a lodge, cabins, RV sites and a KOA campground. Costanoa's location is spectacular, wedged between the Pacific Ocean to the west and hills to the east. There are hiking trails that will take you in either direction.

Our tent bungalow was basic, but clean and comfortable. It was a canvas tent built over a frame of 2x4's with a painted plywood floor. Three walls had glass windows and the front had a lockable door. The bungalow contained a queen bed, two small nightstands with lamps, and two chairs. The bed was equipped with a dual control electric blanket, and it was needed. Even though we were there in mid-August, the air off the Pacific was cool. There were two Adirondack chairs outside for seating.

Costanoa has about 85 canvas bungalows for rent and they share three comfort stations. The comfort stations have men's and women's bathroom facilities and showers, along with a sauna and an outdoor fireplace with seating. Bathrobes and towels are provided with your bungalow, but you will want to add a flashlight for walking back and forth after dark.

The bungalows come in several configurations. In addition to the single queen bed, like ours, you can rent a bungalow with a queen and single bed. You can also rent family bungalows where two bungalows are located side by side and can accommodate up to six people with a shared outdoor seating area between the bungalows. Bungalows can be rented with or without hot tub privileges.

A restaurant with a full bar is on site that serves very good food. Their seafood is especially good, and many of the greens they serve are grown organically at Costanoa. The restaurant is open for breakfast, lunch and dinner. A small gift shop next to the restaurant has wines, basic foods and snacks for sale.

Costanoa is open year round.

# Deetjens Big Sur Inn

48865 Highway One
Big Sur, CA 93920
831-667-2377
www.deetjens.com
$$ - $$$$

One of the most scenic drives in the state of California is Highway One heading south from the Monterey Peninsula. The road clings to the steep sides of the Santa Lucia Range and overlooks the Pacific Ocean, which at times is hundreds of feet below the road. The 80-mile stretch of coast from Carmel to Ragged Point is known as the Big Sur. About 30 miles south of Carmel, Deetjens Big Sur Inn occupies a small canyon cut back into the hills.

Helmut Deetjen came to the Big Sur in the 1930's and bought 120 acres of land in Castro Canyon. Before Highway One was completed in 1937, Castro Canyon was a traditional overnight stop on the coastal wagon route. Deetjen began welcoming travelers.

Helmuth built Norwegian-style cabins and rooms over the years. They were built of scavenged redwood, locally milled. When

Helmuth died in 1972, he left the inn, "…to be forever enjoyed by transient guests wanting to experience the peace, friendship and beauty that can be found at the Inn". A Preservation Foundation operates the Inn now.

The accommodations are rustic. Heat comes from fireplaces, wood burning stoves and electric heaters. The hand-hewn doors have no locks or keys (they can be secured from the inside). There are no phones or TV's. The buildings are single wall construction and not soundproof. Children under 12 are allowed only if the family rents both rooms in a two-room building. The buildings are weathered, unpainted wood, and their shapes are sharply angular.

The popular restaurant on the premises serves breakfast and dinner daily in four, intimate rooms. Beer and wine are available accompanying dinner. Weekend stays require a two-night minimum. Deetjens is open year round.

# Dockside Boat and Bed

316 E. Shoreline Drive
Long Beach, CA 90802
800-436-2574   562-436-3111
www.boatandbed.com
Kimberly Harris, Owner
$$$ - $$$$$

Imagine yourself sitting on the deck of your yacht in a comfortable chair with your favorite afternoon beverage in hand. Your view to the west encompasses the Long Beach Lighthouse on the right, the Queen Mary in the distance to your left, and the sun setting into the blue Pacific Ocean center stage. Your contentment gets deeper as you remember that you didn't have to buy your yacht nor maintain it — you are renting it, quite reasonably, by the day.

Dockside Boat and Bed has six yachts, ranging from 38-feet to 54-feet in length, for rent in the heart of Long Beach, California. The yachts occupy all of "D" Dock in Rainbow Harbor. The dock is a wide, modern, floating dock that has propane grills and covered dining tables for renters' use.

The boats all have air-conditioning and heating, nice on-deck seating, comfortable indoors seating, flat screen TV's with DVD's, a galley, one or more heads (bathrooms) and welcoming staterooms. The galleys have coffee makers and coffee, microwaves and refrigerators, as well as glassware, dishes and utensils. A continental breakfast and light snacks are provided. You certainly do not need to cook here, as Rainbow Harbor is located in the midst of over two dozen waterside restaurants that surround your location.

The yachts include:

| | |
|---|---|
| *Obla De Obla Da* | 44' Sundancer |
| *Crown Jewel* | 54' Stevens |
| *Perfect Landing* | 48' Hi-Star |
| *Ranita* | 43' Sea Ranger |
| *Sea Peepers* | 40' Silverton |
| *Fantasea* | 38' Sea Ray |

You will receive an orientation to the boat upon arrival. You cannot drive the yachts as they must stay at the dock, but boat tours are available nearby. Dockside Boat & Bed is open year round and has been in business since 1999.

# Dockside Yacht Lodging

2071 Shelter Island Drive
San Diego, CA 92106
619-333-0104
www.yacht-lodging.com
$$$ - $$$$

If you are visiting San Diego and want something different from a standard hotel room, but with all the amenities, Dockside Yacht Lodging has two yachts for rent to meet your needs. The yachts are located at the Best Western Island Palms Hotel and Marina and guests have full access to the hotel's fitness center, pool and Jacuzzi's. The yachts are five miles from the airport and are convenient to many area restaurants and attractions.

The yachts are air-conditioned, have deck seating, comfortable indoor seating, two flat-screen TV's, staterooms with luxurious linens, fully equipped galleys, glassware, dishes and utensils. The two yachts are:

*Pura Vida*          47' motor yacht
*Narnie O'Shea*      46' sailboat

54

The *Pura Vida* has two staterooms, one with a king bed and one with a queen bed. It has 2.5 baths. The *Narnie O' Shea* has three bedrooms, two with queens and one full. It has two baths. Both yachts have wireless Internet access.

You will receive an orientation to the boat upon arrival. You cannot drive the yachts as they must stay at the dock, but boat tours are available nearby. Dockside Yacht Lodging is open year round and has been in business since 2011.

# East Brother Light Station (Dinner, Bed & Breakfast)

117 Park Place
Richmond, CA 94801
510-233-2385
www.ebls.org
$$$$$

Any lighthouse will offer a water view, but a lighthouse on a small island offers a 360° water view. East Brother Light Station is situated on a small, rock island just off San Pablo Point in the strait that separates San Francisco Bay to the south from San Pablo Bay to the north. Looking south from the island under the Richmond – San Rafael Bridge, you can see San Francisco; to the southwest you can see the tops of the towers of the Golden Gate Bridge.

The East Brother Light Station is unusual in that the light is built into the keeper's house instead of being freestanding. The East Brother keeper's house is a charming clapboard covered, two-story, Victorian home. It was originally designed for each floor to house one light keeper and his family. Today there are two guest rooms, a small gift shop, a large dining room and kitchen on the first floor and two guest rooms, a game room and lounge with fireplace on the second floor. The upstairs rooms each have a private bath and the ground floor rooms share one.

There is a separate, historic foghorn building on the property. All of the old steam equipment still works, and as part of your stay here, the volunteers fire up the boiler in the morning and demonstrate the two-toned horn. There is a fifth guest room with private bath located in the foghorn building.

The lighthouse on East Brother was built in 1873 and had a 4th Order Fresnel lens. The light was automated in 1969. The Coast Guard proposed to demolish the keeper's house and replace it with a pole light. Friends of the lighthouse saved it and have operated the romantic dinner, bed and breakfast there since 1980, with proceeds used to maintain the facility.

The experience at East Brother begins from San Pablo Marina (1900 Western Drive, Richmond), where you are picked up by boat around 4:00 for the 15-minute ride to the island. After a brief tour, guests are free until 5:30, when complimentary champagne and hors d'oeuvres are served. A gourmet dinner follows at 6:30 and includes salad from the on-site organic garden, soup, entrée and dessert with complimentary wine. A hearty breakfast is served at 9:00 the next morning, and you return to the mainland around 10:30.

The island has a 50,000-gallon cistern and a 20,000-gallon above ground water tank. All water is collected from rain. Because of this limited water supply, showers are not available to overnight guests staying only one night. East Brother Light Station operates year round, Thursday through Sunday, each week.

# The Featherbed Railroad

2870 Lakeshore Blvd.
Nice, CA 95464
707-274-8378
www.featherbedrailroad.com
$$$ - $$$$

The Featherbed Railroad sits in a park-like setting on the north shore of Clear Lake, about 175 miles north of San Francisco. There are nine cabooses on the property that have been turned into unique, themed guest cottages. Each caboose retains its historic exterior, original windows and some other original gear, but each one has been decorated to a theme. The themes available are Casablanca, Celebrations, Wine Country, La Loose Caboose, Orient Express, Lovers, Easy Rider, Tropicaboose and Wild Wild West, which we chose.

The Wild Wild West caboose has a curved wooden ceiling and wainscoted walls with wood paneling and dark blue-green wallpaper. The first thing we encountered upon entering the caboose was a western-style saloon bar, complete with a large mirror and old bottles decorating it. The room is decorated with western art, old guns and even a barbed wire sign saying "Howdy". The bed has throw pillows with pictures of wild horses. The bath features a claw-footed tub and shower. The theme is well executed and glances into several of the other cabooses suggested their themes were equally well done.

The grounds have benches for sitting and looking at the lake, and an old British phone booth. Just outside the circle of cabooses is a gas grill, picnic table and comfortable seating area. A small pool and sunning chairs are located near the office. Bicycles for two are available at the office, as are free movies to play on the TV's provided in each caboose.

Each caboose contains a very comprehensive book that provides information on the attractions and restaurants available in the area. We chose to walk just a few blocks along the lakeshore to dine at a lakeside restaurant that was excellent. Breakfast is served in a dining room adjacent to the office each morning between 9:00 and 10:00.

The Featherbed Railroad is open year round.

# Kate's Lazy Desert

58380 Botkin Road
Landers, CA 92285
845-688-7200
www.lazymeadow.com
$$$

Kate's Lazy Desert is located on the High Desert of southern California, about six miles from Joshua Tree National Forest and 15 miles north of Yucca Valley. The lodging at Kate's consists of six vintage Airstream trailers, restored and wildly decorated by the artists Phillip Mayberry and Scott Walker.

Kate, in this case, is Kate Pierson, lead singer for the B-52's. Artists Mayberry and Walker's home is featured in the B-52's award winning video "Love Shack". The Airstreams are each decorated in vivid colors to a theme. Trailers available are named "Tiki", "Lava", "Tinkerbell", "North to Alaska", "Hairstream", and "Planet Air". Each of the trailers has a back-story, and "Hairstream" is decorated with B-52's memorabilia.

The Airstreams were originally located at Lazy Desert's sister property, Kate's Lazy Meadow in New York. After floods on Esopus Creek threatened the trailers three times, they were moved to the High Desert. They are pretty safe from floods now.

Each of the Airstreams sleeps two adults. They are all air-conditioned and have one bedroom and a bath. There is an outdoor swimming pool on the property. The property has incredible desert views and clear, starry nights. A "Hobo Heater", a barrel for burning wood, is available to ward off the chill of the desert nights while stargazing.

Kate's Lazy Desert is open all year except for the month of August.

# Little Red Caboose

45199 Big Oak Lane
Oakhurst, CA
559-760-7607
Rusty Oetinger, Owner
$$

The Little Red Caboose is located on a five-acre property just 20 minutes from the south entrance to Yosemite National Park.

The caboose sleeps up to four people with a queen bed and a sofa bed. The interior features hardwood floors, granite tiles in the bath and granite countertops in the kitchen. The bath has a Jacuzzi tub and a shower. The caboose has a high definition TV with satellite TV and a DVD player.

The kitchen is equipped with a small fridge and freezer, a microwave, and a coffee maker. A propane grill is located on the attached 200 square foot deck, and a table for four with an umbrella is there, as well. The Little Red Caboose is open from April to December currently, but may be open year round in the future.

East Brother Light Station, CA

Treebones Resort camping nest, CA

# Madonna Inn

100 Madonna Road
San Luis Obispo, CA 93405
800-543-9666
www.madonnainn.com
$$$ - $$$$$

The Madonna Inn is internationally known for its themed rooms and full resort services. It is renowned as a romantic destination, but is also child friendly. The rooms are all lavishly furnished and the dining areas are flooded in pink décor.

Alex and Phyllis Madonna started building the Inn in 1954. Alex was travelling a lot, and was not happy with the lodging that was available, so he built a 12-room motel on ten acres of land. He and Phyllis could not agree on how to decorate the rooms, so they named each room and decorated them to match the names. They opened on Christmas Eve 1958 and have been open continuously since.

Today the Madonna Inn has 110 rooms with themes that run from romantic to whimsical. Themes include honeymoon suites,

European-style retreats, Old West, Spanish, Hawaiian, and all-rock rooms with waterfall showers. The rooms are large and generously appointed with couches and plush bedding.

The Inn has a coffee shop, a dining room, a full bar and banquet facilities. It sits on over 1,000 acres and offers horseback riding. The pool has a beach-style entry and accommodates lap swimming. Two hot tubs and a rock waterfall are located at the pool. The spa, fitness center and a pool bar are also in the pool area.

The main bar is done in a traditional dark wood, but the dining room is decorated in hot pink throughout. In the casual coffee shop, the napkins and the sugar for your coffee are pink. The Madonna is known for its elaborately decorated cakes, which are for sale in the coffee shop.

The men's room at the Madonna is infamous for its urinal. The urinal is a trench style, constructed entirely of rocks. As a man steps up to use it, a motion activated waterfall cascades over the rocks to wash the urinal. It is common to see several men standing guard at the door of the room while their wives go inside to see this unique fixture.

The Madonna Inn is open year round.

# Not-A-Bank

26975 Shoreline Highway (Coastal Route One)
Tomales, CA 94971
415-497-9303
Bert Crews, Owner
$$$$

Not-A-Bank is a B & B that is located in a building that formerly was occupied by a bank. The impressive, two-story, stone building was built in 1920 by the Bank of Italy and replaced a bank building from 1875 that was destroyed in a fire. The building sits in the heart of Tomales, a small former railroad town in Marin County.

The Not-A-Bank interior retains many of the bank's furnishings. The concrete bank vault and door are still in place. The full customer counter made of dark wood, etched glass panels and barred teller windows are still intact. The interior also maintains its two-story ceiling. Two large windows face out from the front of the building.

Not-A-Bank's amenities include a king bed, a folding futon-couch, a single bath and shower, a full kitchen, a gas fireplace, both a baby grand piano and a Hammond organ, a TV with DVD, and overstuffed chairs. A continental breakfast is provided.

Tomales is a picturesque, historic town. A number of restaurants are located on its main street. Several movies have been shot in the town and nearby, including the 1990's remake of "Village of the Damned", starring Christopher Reeves and Alfred Hitchcock's "The Birds".

# The Old Albion School

3930 Albion Little River Road
Albion, CA 95410
707-357-1255
www.schoolhouseproperties.com
$$$$$

The Albion Schoolhouse was built by the Albion Lumber Company in 1924 and served as the town school until 1968. After passing through several uses as a community center and shelter for seven Hell's Angels, the property was purchased by record producer Bill Bottrell in 1995. He renovated the building as a home for his family, and eventually moved his studio there. Renowned artists, including Sheryl Crow, Seal, and Tom Petty and the Heartbreakers, recorded there.

The schoolhouse today has three bedrooms for overnight guests and specializes in weddings, parties, retreats, seminars, meetings and vacations in its large facility. Many specialty services are available for guests, including chef services, massages, manicure/pedicures, local wine tastings, ballroom dance lessons and dinner cruises on the Albion River.

Entering the main door, the room on the left marked "Principal's Office" houses one bedroom. Two more bedrooms are located down the hallway to the right. Straight ahead is a large room that was the former library. It has wood floors, large windows, a small stage at one end, bookshelves and a seating area with two couches. This room can be set up in a variety of ways for banquets and meetings.

At the far left of the building in the front is a comfortable lounge with a bar, fireplace and seating area. To the left rear of the building is a large, tiled bathroom with two sinks and a claw-footed tub and shower.

The Old Albion Schoolhouse is open year round.

# Palm Springs Rendezvous

1420 North Indian Canyon Drive
Palm Springs, CA 92262
800-485-2808   760-320-5308
www.palmspringsrendezvous,com
$$ - $$$

When we stepped through the custom-frosted doors of the Palm Springs Rendezvous, we stepped through a time portal into the 1950's. We walked into the open central courtyard and were greeted by 1950's music in the air and the sight of the clear water of the pool, blue outdoor carpet and lounge chairs that said, "Be cool; relax."

The Rendezvous is located in the "uptown" section of Palm Springs about a half-mile from the lively restaurant district. The hotel opened in 1938 as the Loma Linda. It expanded to its present footprint in 1950. The Rendezvous has a typical Palm Springs one-story architecture with a Bermuda-style roof. It surrounds a quadrangle courtyard with a pool, hot tub and bar. All ten rooms open into the courtyard.

The hotel was a favorite haunt of several Hollywood stars during the 1950's. Veronica Lake, Gloria Swanson and Hugh O'Brien stayed here. Marilyn Monroe was a frequent guest and had a favorite room she always stayed in. The hotel adopted its 1950's theme in 1999 and has maintained it through four ownership changes. The staff members, and sometimes the guests, dress in 1950's styles. The hotel was extensively remodeled in 2008.

All ten of the Rendezvous' rooms have king beds, flat screen TV's with DVD players, chairs and a table, small fridge and microwave. The fridge has complimentary soft drinks and a bag of ice cubes, refreshed daily. Each room is decorated to a 1950's theme. We stayed in the "Rebel Without a Cause" room, decorated with James Dean movie posters and pictures. The DVD's of "Giant" and "Rebel Without a Cause" awaited us.

The other themes available include "Hawaiian Surf", "Crooners", "Pretty in Pink" (Marilyn Monroe's room), "Silver Screen", "Stagecoach", "Route 66", "Honeymoon Hideaway", "TV Shows", and "Shake, Rattle & Roll". Each room has DVD's appropriate to its theme, and additional DVD's are available in the breakfast room/lounge.

Breakfast is served either at 8:30 or 10:00, at the guests' choice. The meal starts with a smoothie, followed by fruit, and then the main course. Guests sit at 1950's style tables in the art deco room. Each afternoon at five, the Rendezvous serves complimentary cocktails and hors d'oeuvres poolside. The cocktail of the day is at the whimsy of the staff, but is always cool and colorful. The Rendezvous is open year round.

# The Queen Mary

1126 Queens Highway
Long Beach, CA 90802
877-342-0742
www.queenmary.com
$$ - $$$$

The *Queen Mary* was the fastest and most luxurious passenger ship afloat when she began trans-Atlantic service in May of 1936. She was known as the "Ship of Wood" because of all the exotic woods used in her generous appointments. World War II interrupted her passenger service in September of 1939. She was stripped of all her luxury and converted to a troop carrier. Painted gray, she was known as the "gray ghost" as she carried up to 16,000 troops at a time across the ocean at a speed of 30 knots.

After the war, and a ten-month retrofit, she returned to regular passenger service in July of 1947 and continued that service for twenty years. Her last voyage, her 1,001[st] trans-Atlantic trip, brought her to Long Beach in December of 1967.

The *Queen Mary* is a unique hotel today. You can stay in one of her 346 former First Class Staterooms or one of nine Suites. No two rooms are alike, but all are decorated in her art deco style, have rich wood paneling, operable portholes, and some have original artwork. Some of the staterooms have been joined into two stateroom Family Rooms.

The ship offers guided tours, a fitness center, business center, spa, shops, Wi-Fi, air-conditioning and heating, and flat-screen TV's. The *Queen Mary* is open year-round.

# Railroad Park Resort

100 Railroad Park Road
Dunsmuir, CA 96025
530-235-4440
www.rrpark.com
$$

The Railroad Park Resort is nestled in a quiet valley outside of Dunsmuir, California with a magnificent view of the surrounding mountains. Dunsmuir was historically an important rail center. In 1968, a local family decided to preserve this railroad heritage by turning cabooses into lodging units.

Railroad Park has 23 cabooses, four rustic cabins and an RV park for lodging. The caboose we stayed in had a beautifully finished knotty pine interior, and a large bath with shower. It was the only caboose we stayed at that featured a king bed. The caboose was furnished with a small table and two chairs, a coffee maker and a TV. All the cabooses are air-conditioned.

The park offers quite a bit to see by wandering the grounds. A 1927 steam locomotive and its coal car are parked next to a watering tank. Behind the office are two restored dining cars that are open from 4:00 to 9:00 Wednesday through Sunday for drinks and dinner. A massive, old wooden railroad snowplow, a deteriorating flatcar and a track clearing work car are scattered around the property.

A nice pool, hot tub and picnic area are located in the center of the park. The Railroad Park Resort is open year round.

# Santa Barbara Autocamp

2717 De La Vina Street
Santa Barbara, CA 93105
888-405-7553
www.sbautocamp.com
$$ - $$$

The Santa Barbara Autocamp began in 1922, and today offers guests the opportunity to stay in one of five restored, vintage Airstream trailers. The camp was the idea of an enterprising city council member who convinced the city that offering travelers a place to camp for the night near stores and restaurants would be good for the city's business community.

The Autocamp's five Airstreams are sited in a cluster of oak trees in a shaded grass area at the entry to the camp. Each site has an awning extending from the Airstream, a wood deck, two Adirondack chairs, an electric grill and two vintage beach cruiser bicycles for guest use. The State Street downtown-shopping district is an easy bike ride from the camp. The Airstreams have different bed configurations, but all were clean and had flat screen TV's and a full kitchen with complimentary coffee and tea. The Autocamp's literature states, "Our goal is to honor the authenticity of the past." The Autocamp is open year round.

Santa Barbara Auto Camp, CA

Dockside Boat & Bed, CA

# Tin Lizzie Inn

7730 Laurel Way (P. O. Box 63)
Fishcamp, CA 93623
559-641-7731 May – Oct   661-513-0524 Nov – Apr
www.tinlizzieinn.com
Dave & Sheran Woodworth, Owners
$$$$$

The Tin Lizzie Inn is located just two miles south of the south entrance to Yosemite National Park. The inn is an elegant, 1890's style Victorian bed and breakfast, but it was built in 2006. Modern construction means modern wiring, plumbing, heating and air-conditioning, but the 1890's styling is authenticated by the use of many antique elements. You will find elegant moldings and woodwork throughout, original stained-glass windows, fireplace mantels, door hardware, antique lighting fixtures, marble sinks and pull-chain toilets. But the fireplaces are gas, and there are flat screen TV's in the rooms.

The name Tin Lizzie Inn comes from the affectionate nickname for the Model T Ford, and every guest at the Tin Lizzie gets a tour of Fishcamp riding in Dave's 1915 Model T Ford. The Model T had three pedals on the floor and the accelerator on the steering column. If you like, Dave will let you take a turn behind the wheel and we can attest that driving a Model T is a hoot!

Two B & B suites are located upstairs in the house. Both of them are very private. They have king beds, comfortable seating areas in front of the fireplaces, and large baths with heated floors and air-jetted tubs. A gourmet breakfast is provided with your stay each morning.

A four-bedroom vacation cottage is located across the street from the Inn. It has a large living area, a dining area and a full kitchen. It would be a great place for four couples or a family to be together and use it as a base to explore Yosemite Park.

And if you are going to explore the park, consider doing it in a Model A Ford. Dave and Sheran have three of them and you can add rental of a Model A onto your room rental. Traffic through Yosemite is slow during the summer anyway, so the Model A would be perfect for this drive.

Dave is a collector of all things old. Do get him to talk about his collections. The Tin Lizzie Inn is open year round.

# Treebones Resort

71895 Highway One
Big Sur, CA 93920
877-424-4787
www.treebonesresort.com
Tom & Corinne Handy, Owners
$$$$$

Treebones Resort offers lodging in a luxury yurt village perched on a ridge of the Los Padres National Forest overlooking the Pacific Ocean with expansive ocean and coastal mountain views. The resort is the brainchild of John and Corinne Handy, who purchased the triangle shaped property in 1987 and created the village. In the 1960's, local hippies affectionately named the area Treebones because of the silvery appearance of the native dead cedar trees as they bleached from the sun.

The resort has 16 yurts in its village and seven campsites. Each yurt is constructed on a wooden deck. The canvas structures have a sky dome in the center of the cone-shaped roof. Each is furnished with a queen bed, night tables and lamps, a space heater, a table and two chairs, and a sink with hot and cold water. The floors are pine, and the walls are canvas, and not that soundproof. You will hear birds, wind, rain, and maybe even your neighbors.

Baths and showers are shared and are located in the lodge a few minutes walk away. The lodge houses a convenience and gift shop and is where the self-serve breakfast is available each morning. The lodge restaurant is open for lunch and dinner. The Wild Coast Restaurant sushi bar is open most evenings and has an ocean view. Outside the lodge is a deck for dining that looks out on the Pacific Ocean. The pool and hot tub are open from 9:00AM to 9:00PM each day.

Treebones also offers a unique campsite that comes with a "human nest" available for adventurous guests' lodging. The nest is made of willow branches and sits on a bluff overlooking the Pacific. The willow branches define the nest, but they do not protect you from the elements completely. You need to bring a tent in case the weather doesn't cooperate. The stay in the nest is a camping experience and you need to bring all your own gear.

Treebones Resort is off the grid. The resort produces its own electricity for light loads and does extensive recycling. An organic garden provides fresh greens and herbs for the restaurant. It is truly a village, as the Handy family and all twenty of their full time staff live there.

Treebones Resort is open year round.

# The Victorian Mansion

326 Bell Street
Los Alamos, CA 93440
805-344-1300
www.thevick.com
Rod Rigole, Proprietor
$$$$$

The Victorian Mansion at Los Alamos has the most elaborately done themed rooms of any place we stayed in the US. The length the Vick has gone to in order to immerse guests in their themes is extraordinary. It is truly an eclectic B & B.

The mansion was originally built in 1864 in Nipomo. In 1980, it was moved to its present location. Two hundred artists, sculptors and craftsmen then worked on the structure for almost ten years transforming it. Muralist Joyce Ortner alone spent two years, forty hours a week, creating murals on every wall of the suites. The Vick opened as a B & B in 1989.

There are six suites and their themes are "Gypsy", "Pirate", "French", "Egyptian", "Roman", and "The 50's". When you enter the suites, the four wall murals and the furnishings put you into the theme. Each suite contains a deep, soaking hot tub. Neither the bathroom nor the closet is visible at first, as all are hidden from view by elements of the decorations. All of the suites have flat screen TV's and DVD's with movies appropriate to the theme included. Also included with your suite is a complimentary bottle of wine, as you are in the wine country area made famous in the movie "Sideways".

We stayed in the Gypsy Suite. Our four walls were decorated in murals of the mountains of Eastern Europe in the four seasons. Our bed was in a Gypsy wagon, our hot tub was constructed of mountain stone, and our dining table was made to look like a Gypsy caravan wheel overlaid with stained glass.

All of the suites were exceptionally well executed. The 50's suite has the bed in a 1956 Cadillac convertible, parked at a drive-in movie with a projector screen TV. The Pirate suite has the bed in the Captain's quarters of a ship and the lamps sway mechanically to simulate the rolling of the ship. The French suite has its bed in a loft overlooking Paris. The Roman suite bed is in a chariot.

Breakfast is served en suite via a hidden dumb waiter passage at a time of your choosing. Restaurants are located nearby for dinner. The Vick serves adults over 21, and is open year round.

Two more suites are planned for the future. One will be built in the structure of a 1914 yawl, which is already on the premises. The other will be a tree house.

# Wigwam Village #7

2728 W. Foothill Blvd
Rialto (San Bernardino), CA 92410
909-875-3005
www.wigwammotel.com
$

Wigwam Motel #7 was the last, and possibly the best known, of seven Wigwam Villages that were built in the United States between 1933 and 1949. In 1933, Frank Redford built a tepee shaped building to house his collection of Native-American artifacts as both a museum and shop. He was supposedly inspired by an ice cream store he saw that was shaped like an ice cream cone that had been dropped upside down. The following year he built a few more such structures to encourage visitors to spend the night. In 1936, he was granted a patent for his Wigwam Motel concept.

Wigwam Motel #7 is in the best condition of the three villages that remain, and the only one with a pool. It is, and has always been, located on historic Route 66 in San Bernardino, but somewhere along the way acquired a Rialto address.

The Pixar movie "Cars" celebrated Route 66 culture. In that movie, Wigwam Motel #7 is depicted as the "Cozy Cone Motel", a mixture of the Wigwam Motel, the Blue Swallow Inn (New Mexico), and Ray's Café.

Wigwam Motel #7 consists of 20 wigwams; 19 of them are available for guest lodging. All have been recently refurbished inside and out. The 30-foot tall, stuccoe exteriors look great. The interiors have queen beds or two twin beds, two overstuffed chairs or a couch, a small refrigerator, and a flat screen TV. The floors are carpeted.

The central area inside of the circle of wigwams is a well maintained yard surrounding a well kept up, kidney-shaped pool. An outdoor grill there is available for guest use.

The owners are notably friendly and the rates are a bargain. The Wigwam Motel is listed on the National Register of Historic Places and is open year round.

# Best Western Movie Manor

2830 U. S. Hwy 160 W
Monte Vista, CO 81144
800-771-9468   719-852-5921
$ - $$

The Best Western Movie Manor is located on the south side of Highway 160, two miles west of Monte Vista, Colorado. Its 54 rooms are set on two floors of a building with a slight dogleg angle to it. Each room has a picture window facing to the east, and the motel comprises the western border of the historic Star Drive-in Theater. Most rooms have a good view of the drive-in screens.

The Star Drive-in has two screens and shows two movies nightly, and simultaneously. An in-room speaker can play the audio from Screen 1, and you can listen to the audio from Screen 2 on the radio at 88.1 FM.

The rooms are standard Best Western. All of the rooms are named after movie stars and the rooms are decorated with movie posters. A fitness room is available to all guests. A complimentary breakfast is served in the morning. Kelloff's Restaurant is located on site and serves dinner each evening.

If you are making a reservation in order to watch a movie, be sure to ask for a good view of the screen in the special request section of the online reservation form. Frequent customers know to do this to secure the rooms with the best view. While you are watching the movie, you can stroll over to the snack bar at the drive-in and purchase some real movie popcorn to take back to your room.

The overall movie experience is just OK. The rooms are better oriented for watching Screen 1 than Screen 2, and both screens are a bit far away. You will have trouble reading any sub-titles on the screen. The in-room audio competes with the noise from the standard wall air-conditioner. But it is still pretty cool to lie in bed watching a movie and snacking on popcorn that is the real deal!

# Castle Marne
# Bed and Breakfast Inn

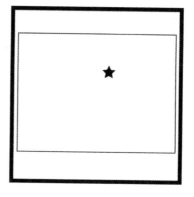

1572 Race Street
Denver, CO 80206
303-331-0621
www.castlemarne.com
$$ - $$$$$

Castle Marne occupies a three-story, stone building that was constructed in 1889 as a private residence for Wilbur Raymond. Renowned architect William Lang, who designed over 300 Denver homes and other buildings, including the Unsinkable Molly Brown's, was the architect of the Raymond house. Lang designed a signature stained glass window into all his buildings, and the six-foot stained glass "Peacock" window dominates the landing of the stairway to the second floor in Castle Marne.

The Castle is constructed of 22-inch thick, intricately carved, Rhyolite lavastone that is multi-colored and sparkles in the sun. The interior boasts elaborate woodwork, particularly in the entry hall and in the mantle of the fireplace in the main floor parlor room.

The building was originally known as the Raymond House for its first owner, but quickly served as a private residence for a succession of owners. Phillip Van Cise, who purchased the home in 1918, named the home the Marne, because he fought in the Battle of the Marne in WWI, and the building reminded him of the manor homes along the River Marne.

Jim and Diane Peiker purchased the castle in 1988 and renovated it with daughter and son-in-law Louie and Melissa Fehér-Peiker. Guests can look through photo albums of the extensive renovation in the parlor. It opened as the Castle Marne Bed & Breakfast Inn in 1989 on the house's 100th birthday, and has been operated by the family since then. There are nine guest rooms, all tastefully decorated in a Victorian style. Three of the rooms have two-person hot tubs located on private balconies. Other rooms have Jacuzzi tubs and three rooms have original claw-footed tubs with shower rings.

The innkeepers are very friendly and deliver a first class service. Afternoon tea and sweets are served at four-thirty each day, and "sleepy time" teas and cookies are put out in the parlor at eight-thirty. The Marne is located in the historic Wyman District of Denver and a number of well-reviewed restaurants are within easy walking distance.

There are two breakfast seatings, at 7:00 and 8:30 weekdays and at 8:00 and 9:30 on weekends. Breakfast consists of fresh baked muffins, juice (including the Castle's signature orange and cranberry blend), a fruit medley, fresh baked bread, an entrée, a private coffee blend and tea. Breakfast is served in the original formal "Peacock" dining room.

The Castle Marne is listed on the DuPont Registry of American Castles and the National Registry of Historic Places. It is open year round.

# Jersey Jim Lookout Tower

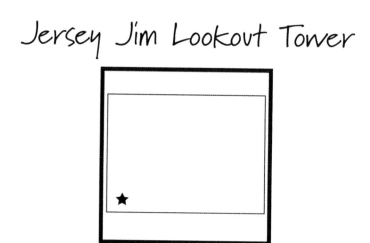

Jersey Jim Foundation
P. O. Box 1032
Mancos, CO 81328
970-533-7060
www.firelookout.org/cohost-co/jerseyjim.html
$

The Jersey Jim Lookout Tower is located in southwestern Colorado about 14 miles north of the town of Mancos on Forest Road 561. The road is accessible by two wheel drive vehicles. The tower is named after a local cattle rancher who raised Jersey cows.

The Forest Service built a log tower at this location in 1942 and erected the present tower in 1964. The tower was in use into the 1970's. In 1991, the tower was saved from destruction and was remodeled by the Jersey Jim Foundation, which owns it today. All rental income is earmarked for preserving the tower.

The 54-foot tower sits at 9,830 feet of elevation in the San Juan National Forest. A 15' by 15' cabin is at the top. The cabin is furnished with a double bed, a table for four, propane heat and light, and a sink. There is no electric or running water. Some of the original furnishings are in the cabin, including the circular fire finder used by the Forest Service to pinpoint fire locations.

Guests must bring their own food, water for cooking and washing, bedding, garbage bags and flashlights. The tower has a hoist that can be used to bring food, water and gear up to the cabin level in loads weighing less than 20 pounds each. A pit toilet and a charcoal grill are located at the base of the tower. Guests are expected to clean the cabin upon leaving and to take out all of their garbage.

The tower is available for rent from late May through mid-October. Reservations are taken by phone beginning with the first business day in March. It is common for the entire season to book up within that first week.

# The Wyman Hotel & Inn

Greene & 14th Street
Silverton, CO 81433
800-609-7845
www.thewyman.com
Roger & Tana Wrublik, Innkeepers
$$$ - $$$$

The Wyman Hotel occupies a corner lot in the center of Silverton, Colorado, a mountain community with a colorful past to explore while visiting. The hotel has 17 guest rooms inside the 1902, redstone building. In addition to the hotel rooms, the Wyman offers a single caboose for guests in a courtyard adjacent to the hotel.

The caboose is a bay window model that ran on the Southern Pacific line. It serves as a romantic getaway and is one of the few cabooses we stayed in that has a whirlpool tub inside, located at the bay windows. The caboose has an antique full bed, a pot-bellied stove, a bathroom, a small fridge, a coffeemaker and a couple of chairs. The caboose is not air-conditioned, nor is the hotel, but the 9,315-foot elevation makes air-conditioning unnecessary.

The hotel is decorated with antiques and pictures of early Silverton in its hallways. Room doors are left open until guests check in, so early guests are free to wander the hotel looking at the different decors. Tana bakes cakes and cookies for the afternoon tea, and sets out wine and cheese for a cocktail hour from 5:00 to 6:00.

The Wyman is a B & B and breakfast is served at 8:00 in the dining room each morning. You can ask for a private table or can sit with other guests, as you choose. The menu varies each day, and is a delicious full meal.

Silverton is a small city. There are a number of restaurants and shops available within easy walking distance and there are many things to do in the area. If you arrive for your stay on the historic Durango & Silverton Rail Road, used for filming the train scenes in "Butch Cassidy and the Sundance Kid", the Wyman will arrange transportation to and from the hotel.

The Wyman Hotel & Inn is open year round.

# Winvian

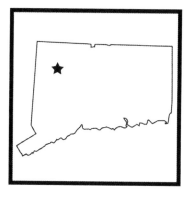

155 Alain White Road
Morris, CT 06763
860-567-9600
www.winvian.com
$$$$$+

Winvian sits on 113 acres of partially wooded land in the scenic Litchfield Hills of western Connecticut. Winvian offers 19 cottages with different themes that are the height of whimsical luxury. In addition to the lodging, there is a spa on premises, as well as a gourmet restaurant with an extensive wine cellar.

Winvian's 19 cottages are each decorated to a theme. The themes available are Log Cabin, Music, Beaver Lodge, Treehouse, Woodlands, Maritime, Secret Society, Golf, Library, Stone, Charter Oak, Camping, Industry, Greenhouse, Connecticut Yankee, Artist, Helicopter, Hadley Suite and Stable. In the helicopter suite, the sleeping area is actually inside a Sikorsky helicopter.

We walked the idyllic property when we visited here, but were unable to see the interiors in person because they were occupied.

Everything about Winvian speaks to a well-executed experience that we have no doubt would be extraordinary.

There are different prices for weekdays and weekends. The a la carte prices include breakfast. There are also packages available that include all meals and drinks, spa visits and other activities. Winvian is open year round.

# Jules Undersea Lodge

51 Shoreland Drive
Key Largo, FL 33037
305-451-2353
www.jul.com
$$$$$

The Jules Undersea Lodge is a one-of-a-kind lodging, and an outrageously quirky sleep. It offers the only opportunity in the United States to spend the night under the sea, gazing out through a 42" round window at the water world on the other side. And you can have a pizza delivered for dinner!

The lodging facility was originally built as the La Chalupa Research Lab and it was placed off the coast of Puerto Rico in 100 feet of water. Over 25 years ago, owner Ian Koblick, an expert on undersea habitation, moved the lab to the Emerald Lagoon on Key Largo and began offering overnight lodging.

The lodge has three main rooms. An 8-foot by 20-foot common area houses the galley, dining and entertainment center. You will find a well-stocked kitchen, books, music and movies here. At the other end, another 8-foot by 20-foot room has been partitioned into two private bedrooms. Each 8-foot by 10-foot bedroom has a mini-fridge, sink, and entertainment center with a VCR/DVD system. But the main attraction in the bedroom is the 42" round window.

Between these two rooms is the wet room where you enter the lodge by SCUBA diving under the facility and coming up into a 5 by 7-foot "moon pool". You will leave your dive gear in the wet room and take a hot shower before entering the living areas. The shared bathroom is also located in this room.

The lodge is monitored 24 hours a day by your mission director. An umbilical cord provides fresh air, water, power and communications to the submerged lodge. There is a telephone and intercom in each bedroom and the galley. The galley also has a marine radio.

You need to SCUBA down 25 feet to enter the lodge, but you do not need to be a certified diver to stay here. There is a three-hour class for non-divers that will teach you what you need to know in order to dive to the lodge with the Jules Lodge certified instructors.

The lodge is normally occupied by two couples, but can be rented privately. You need to be in good health to stay here. The lodge is closed during the coldest months of the year.

# The Rock Ranch

5020 Barnesville Hwy (GPS use 5020 Hwy 36)
The Rock, GA 30285
www.therockranch.com
$

The Rock Ranch is a working cattle farm located about an hour south of Atlanta. It is owned by S. Truett Cathy, the founder of restaurant chain Chic-Fil-A, and is dedicated to "Growing healthy families".

The Rock Ranch offers group lodging in eight Conestoga Wagons. Each Conestoga houses eight people in four sets of bunk beds. The Conestoga's are available for groups from eight to 64 guests. If more than 64 guests are coming, space is available to pitch tents.

The ranch offers cane-pole fishing, hayrides, paddleboats, train rides, zip lines and a petting zoo. Groups can also arrange for a hot dog dinner, a storyteller or an astronomer for your outing.

The ranch is open year round.

Heliohouse Earthship, NM

Izaak Walton Inn Locomotive, MT

# Dog Bark Park Inn

2421 Business Loop 95
Cottonwood, ID 83522
208-962-3647
www.dogbarkparkinn.com
Dennis Sullivan & Frances Conklin, Owners
$

It is impossible to not notice the 30-foot tall beagle "Sweet Willy" and 12-foot tall pup "Toby" standing beside the road on the north side of Cottonwood, Idaho. The two giant beagles are the creation of chainsaw carving artists Dennis and Frances and sit in the yard beside their studio and gallery. Sweet Willy is a B & B that can sleep four people.

Dennis Sullivan was just getting by as a carver of wooden dogs in 1995 when the QVC Shopping Channel aired a promotion called "50 in 50". Over 50 weeks, QVC highlighted twenty local manufacturers in all 50 states, one state per week. Dennis qualified for Idaho, and after the show aired, he was a hit. He sold 10,000 dogs, and spent the next 18 months filling the orders. With this business success, he and Frances got married.

One night over dinner, they discussed building a large dog to attract customers to their business. One thing led to another, the scheme got grander, and by the end of the meal and a bottle of wine, the Dog Bark Park Inn idea was born.

You enter "Sweet Willy" at the shoulder from a second floor deck. A spacious bedroom with a queen bed and sitting room with a small fridge, microwave and coffee pot, is located near the front legs. The bathroom, appropriately, is located in the rear. There is a charming room in the dog's head, which is reached by a ladder. It can be used as a sitting room, and two futon mattresses provide a place for two more guests to sleep.

The lodging is air-conditioned. There is no TV. You can browse the gallery next door to see the many carved dog offerings for sale. You can even purchase a souvenir book titled, "Sweet Willy – A Noble and Absurd Undertaking". The Dog Bark Park Inn is open year round.

# Wildlife Prairie Park

3826 N. Taylor Road
Hanna City, IL 61536
309-676-0998
www.wildlifeprairiestatepark.org
$ - $$

Wildlife Prairie Park is located near Peoria, Illinois. It was founded in 1978 by William and Hazel Rutherford and is situated on 2,000 acres of land that was partially strip-mined. The park was gifted to the State of Illinois in 2000 and receives about 150,000 visitors annually.

The park is home to over 50 animal species that are native to Illinois. Many of the species are currently listed as endangered. The park houses badgers, bison, black bear, cougar, coyotes, deer, elk, fox, wolves, otters, hawks, owls and eagles, among other species. Easy hiking trails allow you to walk past their habitat areas. You can also take a 20-minute safari jeep ride through the bison and elk ranges.

The park is very child-friendly. A 24-inch narrow gauge railroad train will take you on a 30-minute ride through a portion of the park. There is a large playground that features a 58-foot tall slide, along with other playground equipment.

The park is open from 9:00 to 6:30. Overnight guests stay within the park and are given a special gate code to access the park lodging after hours. There are several quirky lodging choices available. We stayed in prairie stables — rather conventional hotel-type rooms made to look like a converted stables — that sleep four. There is a 30-year-old log cabin overlooking a wooded area from a hill. The lake cottages are round structures that look like old grain silos that sleep three. And finally, there are four cabooses that sleep up to four adults and two children.

The park is open year round.

# William M. Black
# Boat & Breakfast

National Mississippi River Museum & Aquarium
350 East Third Street
Dubuque, IA 52001
800-226-3369 x 213   563-557-9545 x 213
www.rivermuseum.com/groups_overnight.cfm
$

The William M. Black was a state of the art, steam powered dredge when it was built in 1934, just before diesel power replaced steam. The ship is 277 feet long, 85 feet wide and displaces 1,700 tons. She is powered by two 600 HP steam engines turning side paddles and making 10 MPH at full steam. She operated for 39 years between 1934 and 1973 on the Missouri River. In fact, she dredged the original shipping channel on the Missouri.

Today the William M. Black is permanently parked at the Mississippi River Museum in Dubuque, Iowa and offers the opportunity for groups to stay aboard the historic ship. The minimum size group is 15 people and the maximum is 55. Guests can either bring their own linens/sleeping bags or can rent linens for a small fee. There are 32 open bunks in the Crews' Quarters in the back of the dredge. Smaller rooms with similar bunks handle more guests. There are two bathrooms in the Crews' Quarters, each with three flush toilets, three sinks and two showers. Several of the smaller rooms have shared bathrooms at the end of the hallways.

An overnight stay includes admission to the museum and breakfast in the National River Center Café. The William Black is open from April through October.

# Jailhouse Inn

601 E. Bridge Street
Elkader, IA 52043
563-580-0041
www.elkaderjailhouseinn.com
Dr. Tim Kane and Julie Carlisle-Kane, Owners

The Jailhouse Inn sits on a three-acre hill looking west over the small town of Elkader, Iowa. The handsome white limestone building was built in 1870, and served as the Clayton County Jail until 2006. The inn consists of two distinct, but joined, structures. The three-story, limestone building was formerly the home of the jailer, the sheriff, and the judge. The rear cellblock building housed the inmates.

The Jailhouse has three suites available for guests, all located in the former jail offices building. The 3rd floor Harstad Suite and the 2nd floor Botanical Suite accommodate two guests. The 2nd floor Emma Big Bear suite consists of two rooms and can accommodate from two to five guests.

The guests' common area is in the former cellblock. There were 12 jail cells on two floors along the length of the large room. A catwalk that provided access to the 2nd floor cells has been removed. The cells are open and are in the condition they were in when the jail closed.

The majority of the room's space is a large open area that contains a comfortable seating area facing a flat screen TV, a dining table and chairs, and a bar. Beer and wine are available for purchase. A wooden shuffleboard court is provided for guest use, as well.

The Turkey River runs through the middle of Elkader, and it is about a six-block walk to the town center. There are a number of interesting shops to browse, and several restaurants that have outdoor seating overlooking the river.

The inn serves breakfast in the common room each morning. Our breakfast included a quiche made with organic veggies that Julie grew in her garden, along with cantaloupe and watermelon from her garden. Julie is a cheerful host and took good care of us. The Inn has been in business since 2008 and is open year round.

# Jailer's Inn Bed & Breakfast

111 West Stephen Foster Avenue
Bardstown, KY 40004
800-948-5551   502-348-5551
www.jailersinn.com
$$ - $$$$

The Jailer's Inn is located in the center of Bardstown, Kentucky, just one-half block from the Courtyard Square. It is surrounded by historic buildings that have been repurposed as restaurants and lodging. The site has served as a jail since 1797. The front of the building, known as the "old jail", was built in 1819. The back of the building, built in 1874, is known as the "new jail". The structures served as the Nelson County Jail until 1987.

The "old jail" building contains six guest rooms plus a family suite with two bedrooms and a living room, all decorated with antiques and heirlooms. All rooms have a private bath. There is also one room in the "new jail" building that allows guests to experience an authentic jail cell. It contains two of the original bunks, but also has a waterbed and private bath. The remainder of the "old jail" is unchanged from its days as an active jail. Guests receive a tour of the jail with their stay.

A large, walled-in courtyard is located in the back of the jail. This courtyard was used in the past for prisoner exercise, as well as the location of the gallows. A full breakfast is served in this area, weather permitting.

The Jailer's Inn Bed & Breakfast is open year round.

# Wigwam Village #2

601 North Dixie Hwy
Cave City, KY 42127
270-773-3381
www.wigwamvillage.com
$

From 1933 to 1949, seven Wigwam Villages were built across the country. Wigwam Village #2 is the oldest of the three remaining wigwam villages, having been built in 1937. It was originally built along the main highway leading to Mammoth Cave, but was bypassed when Interstate 64 was built.

The office and gift shop are housed in a 52' tall wigwam that took 13 tons of steel and 38 tons of concrete to build. When it was built it also housed a restaurant, but the restaurant closed after the Interstate came through.

There are 15 wigwams arranged in a half-circle arrayed around the office. These wigwams are 20' tall and are painted like Native-American tepees. Ten wigwams have one double bed and five have two double beds. All the wigwams have air-conditioning and heat, a private bath with shower, a TV and an in-room coffee maker.

There is a large playground in the center of the wigwam village that includes a 15' by 15' misting deck to keep children cool while they play. An ice machine and soda vending are next to the office. A large picnic shelter and grills are available to guests. Several restaurants are located in nearby Cave City.

Wigwam Village #2 is very child-friendly and is open year round.

# Wildwood Inn
# Tropical Dome & Themed Suites

7809 US 42
Florence, KY 41042
800-758-2335   859-371-6300
www.wildwood-inn.com
$$$

The Wildwood Inn consists of 27 themed suites, 12 safari huts, a number of regular motel rooms (some with double Jacuzzi tubs) and a tropical domed pool for year round use. There are 14 family-themed suites and 13 romance-themed suites.

The Wildwood has gone through quite an evolution, beginning in 1932 as a one-room cabin for rent. In 1962, the Wildwood added a 32-room motel. In 1978, Wildwood pioneered putting Jacuzzi tubs in their rooms. In 1985, the pool was enclosed as a Tropical Dome for use year round. Themed rooms were started in 1990 and the Wildwood has been consistently adding themed rooms since then.

We were first checked into a Safari Hut, essentially a hard copy of a yurt. However, the air-conditioner was not working. When we pointed this out to the management, we were immediately offered a free upgrade to a themed suite. We chose the Tropical Suite and it was nicely decorated. On the ground floor we had our bed, bathroom, and a sitting area made to look like a beach with lounge chairs and a tiki umbrella table.

An upstairs loft housed a two-person Jacuzzi tub, a table with three chairs, and a Murphy bed. Both the downstairs and the loft had wood floors, bamboo walls, and a painted ocean beach scene with palm trees and sand.

The Tropical Dome contained a large pool with a waterfall you could swim under. A small bar was located adjacent to the pool area and looked cozy. The Wildwood Inn is open year round.

# Keeper's House Inn

Robinson Point Lighthouse Station
P.O. Box 26
Isle au Haut, ME 04645
207-335-2990
www.keepershouse.com
Marshall Chapman, Owner
$$$$$

The Robinson Point Lighthouse Station was built in 1907 to guide fishing boats into the protected Isle au Haut Harbor in bad weather. The lighthouse is owned by the Town of Isle au Haut, is automated and is maintained by the Coast Guard. Marshall Chapman owns the adjacent Keeper's House and operates it as a three-meal B & B.

The Isle au Haut is approximately six miles long by two miles wide. It has a population of about 75 people and is home to a portion of the Acadia National Park. The only access to the island is by way of the mail boat.

Your stay at the Keeper's House starts in Stonington, Maine, where you meet the mail boat for your trip to the island. The boat makes several trips each day, but weather and its cargo load can alter the schedule. The boat stops at the town dock, which is about a one-mile walk from the Inn. It is common for you to travel alongside pallets of supplies for the island's only store and items being shipped to residents. Most of the time the captain will offer to drop you off right at the lighthouse, if you prefer, after the stop in town.

The three-story Keeper's House sits on a rocky bluff looking south over Penobscot Bay and has an uninterrupted view to the west for sunsets. The house has a kitchen, living room and dining room on its ground floor, three nice bedrooms with a shared bath on the second floor, and a garret room with its own bath on the third attic floor. Another room and bath is available in the former oil house. The previous Innkeeper, Jeff Burke, is an artist and many of his portraits decorate the walls.

Marshall owns a Model AA Ford truck that he drives on the island to haul supplies from the town dock to the Inn. He also owns a 1920's Model T Ford that he is converting to electric power.

Dinner, breakfast and lunch are included with your stay, as there are no restaurants on the island. Our dinner consisted of salad, soup, an entrée and dessert, and guests are welcome to bring their own wine. Breakfast included juice, coffee, fresh baked blueberry muffins, and both a vegetarian and seafood quiche. A brown bag lunch contained a wrap, fruit and chips. We hiked into town to catch the mail boat back to the mainland and ate our lunch on the boat. The guests staying for another night were able to take their lunches along on hikes through the national forest.

The Keeper's House is off the grid. They make their own electricity using solar panels, a wind and a propane generator. The electrical supply is limited, so heavy loads like hair dryers are not welcome, but there is plenty of electricity for normal use. Fresh water is made from the sea using reverse osmosis. Water supplies are adequate for short, not lingering, showers.

The Keeper's House Inn is on the National Register of Historic Places and is open each year from Memorial Day weekend through Columbus Day weekend.

# The Norumbega Inn

63 High Street
Camden, ME 04843
877-363-4646   207-236-4646
www.norumbegainn.com
Sue Walso and Phil Crispo, Owners
$$$$ - $$$$$

Joseph Stearns, who invented the duplex telegraph and sold the invention to Western Union, built Norumbega Castle in 1886. He spent a full year touring castles in Europe to obtain design ideas, and incorporated his favorite features into his castle. He built his castle on a hill in Camden, Maine, with a view of the ocean. Camden Harbor is one of the prettiest harbors in Maine.

After Stearns' family died out, the castle passed through several owners, including State Department official Hodding Carter III. In 1984, it became a B & B and continued as one until 2011. By that time, the heirs and trustees of the original B & B owner had allowed the property to become tired.

In March of 2013, Sue Walso and Phil Cristo purchased the Norumbega and have reopened the Inn as a gourmet B & B. They are enthusiastically investing in and restoring the castle to its former glory and improving the 10,000 square foot castle and four-acre grounds. The Inn has 11 guest rooms, including two suites, all with private baths. Most of the rooms have ocean views.

There are four common rooms on the ground floor. The living room, sitting room, dining room and couples' loft all have lovely original woodwork. The fireplaces are magnificent edifices of intricately carved wood and glazed tile.

Phil Crispo is an accomplished chef. He was a chef instructor at the renowned Hyde Park Culinary Institute of America, and he was the winner of an episode of the Food Channel's "Chopped". You will have the opportunity to sample his cooking at breakfast, which is included in your stay. But Chef Phil also offers an optional five-course, fixed-price dinner, and it is well worth it. Each day he searches the local markets for the freshest ingredients and builds the dinner around what he finds. Our dinner was exceptional.

The Norumbega Inn is destined to become a very hot ticket. Its location in Camden provides a number of interesting activities for guests. Sue's personality and enthusiasm will make you as welcome as if you were at home. The rooms and views are first rate. And Chef Phil's cooking will rival the best meals you have had anywhere. The Norumbega is open year round.

# Maine Windjammer Cruises

P. O. Box 617
Camden, ME 04843
800-736-7981   207-236-2938
www.mainewindjammercruises.com
Ray and Ann Williamson, Owners
$$$ - $$$$

Imagine spending several days sailing aboard an authentic, fully renovated, historic coastal schooner among the scenic islands of Maine. After a day moving before the breeze, you will drop anchor in a secluded cove where you can swim, fish, go for a hike ashore, or just relax. The galley provides fresh baked bread, hearty chowders, salads and entrees to keep you fueled. And at night you can marvel at the stars in the sky, far from city lights.

Maine Windjammer Cruises operates three ships out of Camden, Maine from mid-May until early October offering 2, 3, 4, and 5-day cruises. Their ships are:

*Grace Bailey* – built in 1882, she was restored in 1990. The *Grace Bailey* is 123 feet long overall, 81 feet long on deck, and carries 29 passengers. She has 15 cabins and four heads.

*Mercantile* – built in 1916, she was restored in 1992. The *Mercantile* is 115 feet long overall, 80 feet long on deck, and carries 29 passengers. She has 15 cabins and three heads.

*Mistress* – built in 1960, she was restored in 1992. The *Mistress* is 60 feet long overall, 46 feet long on deck, and carries six passengers. She has three cabins, each with its own head.

The ships' cabins are small, but comfortable. Plenty of open deck space is available for you to watch the coastal scenery go by and the ships have large galleys with polished wood tables for meals. The *Grace Bailey* and *Mercantile* are sail powered. The *Mistress* is sail powered, but also motorized.

Anyone over 16 may sail, and children over 12 may sail with a supervising parent. Although the sailing season lasts only the summer, the office is open year-round for information and reservations. You will receive detailed packing and travel information with your reservation confirmation. All meals are included in the price.

# C & O Canal Quarters

1850 Dual Highway, Suite 100
Hagerstown, MD 21740
301-714-2233
www.canaltrust.org
$$

The Chesapeake & Ohio Canal was proposed as early as 1816 as a link between the Ohio River and the Potomac River. Construction started in 1828 and the canal was partially open by 1831. The canal reached Cumberland in 1850 and never went further west as the advent of railroads rendered the canal commercially unfeasible.

Six of the lock houses along the canal have been restored to reflect life on the canal during various historic eras and are available for rent. All of the lock houses are over 170 years old and are listed on the National Register of Historic Places. They are:

Lock house #6 – Restored to the 1950's to tell of the effort to preserve the canal, which was led by Supreme Court Justice William O. Douglas. This lock house has a full kitchen and an indoor bath.

Lock house #10 – Restored to the 1930's to tell about the African American Civil Conservation Corp's restoration work on the canal. This lock house has a full kitchen and indoor bath.

Lock houses #22 & #28 – Restored to the 1830's, reflecting the building and early operation of the canal. These lock houses are rustic with outdoor toilets.

Lock house #25 – Restored to the Civil War era. This lock house is rustic with an outdoor toilet.

Lock house #49 – Restored to the 1900's, the last years of the canal's operations. This lock house has electricity and a stove, but no indoor bath facilities.

Reservations are on a first come, first served basis and can be made twelve months in advance. Only one party at a time is allowed, with a maximum of eight people. A maximum stay of three days is permitted. Lock house #28 requires a ¾ mile walk; all others can be reached by car. You need to bring your own bed linens and bringing your own water is highly recommended. Upon leaving, you need to haul out your trash.

Canal Quarters are available year round.

# The Castle

15925 Mt Savage Road
Mt Savage, MD 21545
3012-264-4645
www.castlebandb.com
Tony and Judi Perino
$$ - $$$

The Castle B & B is nestled in the Appalachian Mountains in far western Maryland near Cumberland and just off the National Road, Route 40. The building is listed on the National Record of Historic Places.

The Castle began in 1840 as a substantial stone house built by the Union Mining Company. In the 1890's, Scottish entrepreneur Andrew Ramsey, the owner of the Mt Savage Enameled Brickworks Company, purchased the home. He converted the stone house into a replica of Craig Castle, a castle that was near his home in Scotland. Ramsey added large verandas and terraces around the house, a third floor, and a kitchen and library wing. He also added a carriage house, a formal garden and a tennis court to the two-acre property. Then he surrounded the property with 16-foot tall stone walls to complete the castle-like appearance.

Ramsey lost his fortune and the castle in the Great Depression. The property served over following decades as a private residence, a dance hall, a brothel, a casino and an apartment building before being purchased by Tony and Judi Perino in 2002. The Castle opened as a renovated B & B in 2004. The Castle has six guest rooms furnished with antiques.

We stayed in the Ramsey Room. This large, second floor room has eight-foot windows that overlook the formal garden. The room has a comfortable sleigh bed, a seating area with couch and chairs, and comes with complimentary sherry. At four in the afternoon, The Castle serves tea and snacks in the parlor.

The upstairs library is a beautiful room. The floor is made of enameled brick. Huge windows overlook the former tennis court on one side, and an enormous fireplace on the opposite side dominates the room. Most of the other floors are made of richly stained wood with intricate patterns.

Our breakfast was served in the dining room, decorated in rich maroon and red colors. The breakfast included coffee and juice, fruit cup and ham and cheese quiche in a house-made pastry crust that was delicious. The Castle B & B is open year round.

# Liberty Fleet of Tall Ships

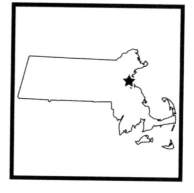

67 Long Wharf
Boston, MA 02110
617-742-0333
www.libertyfleet.com
$ - $$

Liberty Fleet operates what it refers to as a "Boat Hostel" aboard two replica tall ships in Boston Harbor. The *Liberty Clipper* is a replica of the famous clipper ships and the *Liberty Star* is a replica of a coastal schooner. Both ships are sail powered and motorized.

The ships are docked at the New England Aquarium in Boston Harbor. You can check in at the office and drop your bags there as early as 10:00. You will be given a time to board the ship, where you will receive a ship's orientation and be shown to your cabin.

The ships are working ships and are out providing sailing excursions much of the day. Your stay does not include a sail, but overnight guests receive a 30% discount on any sails they book. Only the crew and overnight guests will stay aboard after the last sail of the day. A continental breakfast is provided in the morning at 8:00 AM.

Liberty Fleet's ships are:

*Liberty Clipper* – built in 1983, the *Liberty Clipper* is 125 feet long overall, 86 feet long on deck, and carries 24 passengers. She has 12 cabins, each with a skylight and a sink with hot and cold water. There are three shared heads and three shared showers.

*Liberty Star* – re-built in 2012, the *Liberty Star* is 67 feet long overall, 52 feet long on deck, and carries six passengers. She has three cabins and one shared bath and shower.

Liberty's Boat Hostel is open from June through September.

# The Liberty Hotel

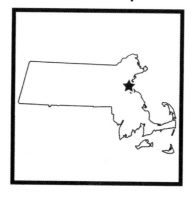

215 Charles Street
Boston, MA 02114
866-961-3778   617-224-4000
www.libertyhotel.com
$$$$$

The Liberty Hotel is a luxury hotel located in the former Charles Street Jail. The magnificent granite building with a 90-foot rotunda was built in 1851 and served as the Suffolk County Jail from then until 1990.

The hotel opened in 2007 with renovations that retained much of the original interior brick walls, iron cell bars and catwalks incorporated into the modern design. The hotel pays homage to the historic nature and use of the building, but in a luxury package. Restaurant venues pick up on the historic theme with names such as "Clink" and "Alibi".

The hotel is located in downtown Boston in the Beacon Hill neighborhood. It is open year round.

Cherry Wood Bed, Breakfast & Barn, WA

Norumbega Inn, ME

SleepAfloat

P. O. Box 961680
Boston, MA 02196
855-343-3456
www.sleepafloat.com
$$$$$

SleepAfloat operates in several cities, primarily on the east coast, offering daily to extended lodging aboard a variety of vessels. A number of the vessels are houseboats, but there are some small yachts, as well. Some of the boats accommodate up to 10 people and work well for group stays and family reunions. SleepAfloat describes their accommodations as "Rooms that Rock!"

SleepAfloat's cities of operations can change over time, so it is best to check their website for current locations. At the time of publication, SleepAfloat was operating in Cape Cod, Baltimore, Boston, Key West, Los Angeles, Miami/Ft Lauderdale, Philadelphia and Washington, D. C.

The number of boats and type of accommodations vary by city. You can get the specifics on their website. Renters must be 25 years of age, but children can be aboard with a supervising parent. Linens and towels are supplied, but there is no daily maid service. They are open year round.

# Starlight Llama
# (Solar) Bed & Breakfast

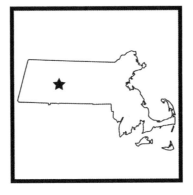

940 Chesterfield Road
Florence, MA 01062
413-584-1703
www.starlightllama.com
John Clapp and Dee Boyle-Clapp

The Starlight Llama Bed and Breakfast is Massachusetts' first solar-powered, off-the-grid, bed and breakfast. The B&B opened in 2008, showcasing the ease of solar-living on a 120-acre farm raising llamas, goats, emus and peacocks. The B&B offers a fresh breakfast that can accommodate gluten-free, vegan and vegetarian diets.

The Starlight Llama has three rooms, each with a bath. The White Room has an en-suite bath, and is the most popular as it is the coolest in the summer. The Pink Room has an en-suite bath and catches the morning sun. The Lavender Room is the largest room and has its bath across the hall. All rooms have queen beds and are decorated with original artwork.

While at the farm, you can hike, bike, snowshoe, walk the trails, and if you'd like, weed a garden, help bring in the hay, or help pound a few handmade nails into John's reproduction Thoreau cabin. Or you can just relax and watch the llamas graze or see the peacocks walk by.

The Starlight Llama Bed & Breakfast is open year round.

# Big Bay Point Lighthouse B & B

#3 Lighthouse Road
Big Bay, MI 49808
906-345-9957
www.bigbaylighthouse.com
$$ - $$$$

The Big Bay Point Lighthouse B & B is located on a 60-foot cliff with a spectacular view over Lake Superior. The lighthouse was built in 1896 and is listed on the National Register of Historic Places. A handsome redbrick building attached to the lighthouse houses the B & B. The facility has been privately owned since 1961 and has been open as a B & B since 1986. There are seven rooms available and a two-night minimum applies on weekends.

The B & B is rather isolated. It is located some 20 miles from Marquette. The B & B serves only breakfast and there are only two small restaurants located in Big Bay itself.

We did not have the opportunity to view the guest rooms. The innkeeper was not helpful and did not want to deal with us, either by phone or in person (He kept pushing us to his website). Even though no guests were present, he was reluctant to let us even view the public rooms.

The Big Bay Lighthouse B & B is adults only and is open year round.

# Jacobsville Lighthouse Inn

38741 Jacobs Street
Lake Linden, MI 49945
906-523-4137
mditty23@netzero.com
$$$ - $$$$

The Jacobsville Lighthouse Inn is located in the ghost town of Jacobsville, about 15 miles south of Lake Linden. The lighthouse marked the way to the dredged channel leading to Houghton and Hancock, Michigan for copper ore freighters.

The original lighthouse, also known as the Portage River Lighthouse, was built in 1855. That lighthouse collapsed and the present lighthouse was built in 1869. The property consists of the lighthouse, an adjacent keeper's house, and an oil house. The light is no longer active.

The property was purchased privately in 1994. The private owners added a wing to the original keeper's house. There are three guest rooms available in the original section of the building, and one of the rooms can sleep four guests. The living and dining room for the B & B are located in the new wing.

Guests can climb the lighthouse and are rewarded with a great view of the waterway looking south. A small deck located at the water's edge provides a more intimate view of the water.

The closest restaurants to the lighthouse are about 15 miles away. The Inn is open year round.

# Middle Island Keeper's Lodge

3550 Rockport Road (GPS)
Alpena, MI
989-884-2722
www.middleislandkeeperslodge.com
Captain Mike Theut
$$$$$

Middle Island sits in Lake Huron about two miles offshore of an abandoned limestone quarry near Alpena. The 265-acre island is uninhabited. Middle Island Lighthouse was activated on June 1, 1905, warning mariners of a dangerous shoal east of the island with its red, 4th Order Fresnel lens. The lighthouse is 71-feet tall and 20-feet in diameter at its base, which has 4' 11" thick walls.

The lighthouse property consists of the lighthouse, the oil house, the keepers' house and the foghorn building. In 2003, the Middle Island Lighthouse Keepers Association remodeled the former foghorn building into a lodge. The lodge sleeps from two to ten people and rents to only one group at a time. One bedroom is on the ground floor. The loft holds two single beds and two bunk beds. A hide-a-bed is located in the living room area.

The lodge is well equipped for a comfortable stay. A large kitchen has a propane stove/oven and a propane refrigerator/freezer. A propane grill is on the outside deck. Plenty of cooking utensils and dishes are available. You need to provide your own food for this island stay, but we found the lodge reasonably stocked with cooking utensils, condiments and water. A large deck wraps around two sides of the lodge and an outdoor shower is located on the deck. The on-demand propane hot water heater worked well and the shower was better than some we've had in motels. The toilet is an outhouse (very clean), so this stay qualifies as somewhat rustic.

The stay at Middle Island is an adventure. The address given above led us, via our GPS, to the beginning of a 3.5-mile gravel road to an abandoned limestone quarry. Capt. Mike met us there in his 19' Mako and transported us to a dock on the west side of the island. He carried our gear to the lodge with a utility vehicle. He offered us a ride, as well, but we chose to walk the 2/3-mile trail. At the lodge, he gave us an orientation and a tour to the top of the lighthouse. Then he left, so we had the island entirely to ourselves.

We enjoyed a relaxing afternoon of hiking trails on the island and reading. After dinner, we walked onto the stone beach and watched the sunset while sitting in front of a roaring driftwood fire set up by Capt. Mike. The Middle Island Keepers Lodge caters to divers and several wrecks are located nearby. The lighthouse is available to guests during the summer months.

# Sand Hills Lighthouse Inn

Five Mile Point Road
P. O. Box 298
Ahmeek, MI 49901
906-337-1744
www.sandhillslighthouseinn.com
Bill & Mary Frabotta
$$$ - $$$$

The Sand Hills Lighthouse is the largest, and the last, manned lighthouse built on the Great Lakes. It was built in 1917 to warn of an offshore shoal in Lake Superior, and housed three lightkeepers and their families. The Coast Guard automated the light in 1939 and it remained active until 1954. During WWII, the property was converted to a training station for the Coast Guard.

Bill and Mary Frabotta bought the property in 1961, and they completely renovated it beginning in 1992. The Inn opened as a B & B in 1995. It is beautifully decorated in a Victorian style and has modern heating, air conditioning and utilities. Since opening as a B & B, one man who was stationed at the lighthouse in 1942 while in the Coast Guard, returns for a visit each year.

The Sand Hills Lighthouse Inn was selected by American Historical Inns as one of the ten most romantic inns in America. It was also recently featured on the Today Show and a PBS special.

The inn has eight guest rooms, each with either a king or a queen bed and a private bath. Breakfast is served each day at 9:30 in the morning. Each evening, a homemade dessert is served in the parlor, where Mary entertains guests by playing the grand piano. The former garage/barracks contains a pool table and games for guests. Guests can also climb to the lighthouse tower to look out onto Lake Superior and watch both sunrises and sunsets.

The Sand Hills Lighthouse Inn is open year round and usually requires a two-night stay from May to October.

# Traverse Tall Ship Company

13390 S. West Bay Shore Drive
Traverse, MI 49684
800-678-0383   271-941-2000
www.tallshipsailing.com
$$$$

The tall ship *Manitou* is one of the largest sailing ships on the Great Lakes. Built in 1983, she is designed as a replica of a typical 1900's era cargo schooner. She is 114 feet in length overall, 72 feet at the waterline and 21 feet wide. She has a 60 passenger sailing capacity and accommodates up to 24 overnight guests in twelve cabins.

Your experience begins when you board ship at 5:30. You are shown to your cabin and given an orientation of the ship. At 6:30, other passengers come aboard for the two-hour sunset cruise and picnic dinner that is included with your stay. You are welcome to help the crew raise the sails, or even assist steering the ship, or you can just enjoy the sail. Beer and wine are available while under sail, but not while at the dock.

When you return to the dock, the sailing passengers and crew depart, but you stay aboard. Since you are docked, you can come and go as you please, should you want to go to town.

The cabins are nicely appointed, but small. Each has comfortable bunk beds and a skylight window that opens for fresh air. If you prefer, you can roll out your sleeping bag on deck and sleep under the stars. There are two shared marine heads aboard. Shore side bathrooms and shower rooms are also available across the street at the office for your use.

The cook comes aboard around 5:00 in the morning to fire up the wood cook stove in the galley. About 7:00, hot coffee, hot chocolate and tea, along with fresh baked muffins, are set out on deck. At 8:00 the ship's bell summons all aboard to gather in the galley at polished wood tables for a full breakfast, all cooked on the wood stove. Our breakfast included fruit and juice, croissants, quiche, bacon, sausage and cheese grits, along with fresh coffee and more muffins.

An adult must accompany children under 18 years of age. The price of your overnight stay includes the sunset sail, picnic dinner and full breakfast. The tall ship Manitou is available for guests from Memorial Day into October.

# Whitefish Point Light Station

18335 N. Whitefish Point Road
Paradise, Mi 49768
888-492-3747
www.shipwreckmuseum.com
$$$

The Whitefish Point light is the oldest operating lighthouse on Lake Superior, in operation since 1849. It is located at the narrowing eastern end of the lake. Over 200 of the 550 known shipwrecks in Lake Superior are located along this stretch of the coast.

The Whitefish Point property is extensive and heavily visited. In addition to the lighthouse, the property includes the former Coast Guard Lifeboat Station Crew Quarters building and the Great Lakes Shipwreck Museum. The location also provides beach access to a swimming beach, for those who are willing to brave the lake's chilly waters.

Five B & B rooms are available for guests in the former Coast Guard Crew Quarters building, constructed in 1923. The B & B was sold out, so we were unable to tour the rooms. The Whitefish Point Light Station is open from May 1 until October 31.

# Wild Cherry RV Resort

8563 E. Horn Road
Lake Leelanau, MI 49653
231-271-5550
www.wildcherryresort.com
$$

The Wild Cherry RV Resort is located on the Leelanau Peninsula, the heart of Michigan's cherry growing region, approximately 15 miles north of Traverse City. The resort is near Leland, Northport and the Leelanau Casino. Cherry orchards, vineyards and 30 acres of woods surround the resort.

The RV Resort has one yurt available to rent. The yurt sits in a secluded wooded location within the resort. The yurt site has a picnic table, fire pit, and charcoal grill. A portable bathroom is located nearby. The yurt is furnished with a queen bed, a twin sized trundle bed, a day bed, and a small table with two chairs. It can sleep four adults or a family of five. The yurt is available with a two-night minimum from about May 1 until September 1.

La Voie Tree House, MN

The Shack Up Inn, MS

# Jailhouse Inn Bed & Breakfast

109 Houston Street, NW
P. O. Box 422
Preston, MN 55965
507-765-2181
www.jailhouseinn.com
Marc & Jeanne Sather
$ - $$$

The Jailhouse Inn occupies a large, Italianate building that was built in 1869. It served as the Filmore County Jail for 102 years, until 1971. Marc and Jeanne Sather remodeled the structure, restoring it to Victorian splendor, and opened their B & B in 1991. Twelve Sheriffs served over the time the structure was a jail and the B & B has twelve rooms, each one named after one of the Sheriffs.

Each of the Inn's rooms is different. Some have fireplaces, some have porches, and others have unique elements associated with their previous function. We chose to spend the night in the former cellblock, named for Sheriff Donald Cook (1947 – 1959). We walked through a conventional privacy door at the end of the hall into the cellblock. Once inside, nothing else was conventional.

The cellblock consisted of four cells, two on each side of a common area, and all behind steel bars. The mechanism for closing the individual cell doors to keep the prisoners in their cells at night still functions, however fire codes prohibit actually closing the doors. Two of the cells contained a queen bed that filled the cell lengthwise, requiring climbing over the bed to get to the far side. One cell had a day bed and a TV. The fourth cell housed the bath and shower. The common area held a hot tub, two over-stuffed chairs, and a sideboard with complimentary sherry. This venue would be great for a family with young children.

The Inn has a kitchen that is open to guests. The refrigerator contains a selection of 50-cent sodas; coffee and tea were also available. Fresh baked cookies were on the counter when we returned from dinner. An honor system wine cooler was available, as well, and we had a glass of wine on a porch that is shared by the guests staying in cellblock and the guests in the former drunk tank.

Coffee was available as early as 7:00 and the full breakfast was served around 8:30. It consisted of fruit, an omelet, fried potatoes with sour cream, and the absolute best cranberry scones we have eaten anywhere. Many of the guests were visiting either to trout fish in the south branch of the Root River, or to bicycle the 60 miles of trails near town. The Inn is open year round.

# LaVoie Tree House

25561 County 11
Long Prairie, MN 56347
320-732-0959
Joyce and Richard LaVoie
$$

The LaVoie Tree House is nestled in the middle of 16 acres of maple and oak forest on the LaVoie's farm. The tree house is a gorgeous, hexagonal, one-room structure made of pinewood, and it has windows on all six walls. The tree house is rustic — there is no electricity and no running water. An outhouse is nearby (very clean), and a chamber pot is provided for those who do not wish to use the outhouse at night.

The tree house is accessed by a stairway, which leads to a deck that wraps around two-thirds of the house. The deck has a small table with two chairs, two recliner lawn chairs and a huge bear-trap for decoration. The interior has a full bed, a small table with two chairs, and two comfortable reading chairs. A number of battery operated lights and oil lamps are provided for lighting at night. A miniature pot-bellied stove sits near the door and firewood is provided. The temperature dropped to 45° the night we stayed here, but we were toasty warm with just a small fire in the early evening to take the chill out of the air.

Everyone who stays at the tree house receives a complimentary tee shirt and guests share a complimentary bottle of red or white wine. Many of the used wine bottles decorate the outhouse, with messages written on the labels by guests telling how much they enjoyed their stay.

Joyce delivers breakfast to the tree house at an agreed upon time. She walks the path to the tree house wearing a bell, to inform guests of her pending arrival. Our breakfast consisted of juice, coffee or tea, fresh fruit, a fresh baked muffin, and "tree bear" porridge, which was wonderful! We lingered on the deck watching the sun filtering through the trees and listening to all the songbirds while we finished our coffees.

The LaVoie Tree House is available year-round, except for December.

# Lighthouse B & B

1 Lighthouse Point
Two Harbors, MN 55616
888-832-5606
www.lighthousebb.org
$$

The Two Harbors Light Station began operation in April of 1892 to guide ships safely into Agate Bay on the north shore of Lake Superior. The original light was a kerosene light inside a 4th order Fresnel lens. The light is now automated and is still an active aid to navigation, making the light the oldest continually operating lighthouse in Minnesota. The light is housed in a 50-foot tall, 12-foot square, red brick tower. The light is 78 feet above the lake surface and is visible for 17 miles.

The Lighthouse B & B, open since 1999, is located in the keepers' house, which is attached to the light tower. The ground floor has a comfortable living room and dining room, both furnished with antiques. The kitchen and office are also on this level. Three guest rooms are on the second floor, along with the shared bathroom. A fourth guest room is available in another building on the lighthouse property.

When we arrived, we were welcomed with an afternoon snack of fresh chocolate cake, which was a nice touch. The lighthouse property has several other structures on it, including a museum in the former foghorn building, and the pilothouse from a wrecked ore freighter, the "Frontenec". The pilothouse holds several navigational displays, as well as some of the ship's original equipment. You can watch ships that are loading taconite ore at the loading docks just west of the lighthouse. The docks load six to eight ships per week.

Our room was quite comfortable, and the shared bath worked well as all the guests were mindful of its shared status. Breakfast was served in the dining room, and it was hearty. The cook joined the guests for coffee after breakfast and was well versed in the history of the lighthouse. The Lighthouse B & B is open year round.

# Northern Rail Traincar Inn

1730 Highway 3
Two Harbors, MN 55615
877-834-0955
www.northernrail.net
Jeff and Cyndi Ryder, Owners
$ - $$$

The Northern Rail Traincar Inn is located just north of Two Harbors, Minnesota and only 25 minutes from Duluth. It sits on 160 acres of wooded property. The lodge consists of ten boxcars, each 50 feet long, and a main building designed to look like a train depot. The ten boxcars are set on two parallel tracks and the area between the cars is an enclosed platform that serves as a central hallway and entry to the boxcars.

The boxcars all have their original exterior, original interior ceiling and other decorative elements. The cars have been made into 17 themed rooms displaying Northwoods, Victorian, Oriental or Safari themes. King Conductor and Queen Conductor rooms utilize an entire boxcar. Porter rooms are built in half a car. Each room is furnished with a TV and is air-conditioned. Some rooms also have a microwave, small fridge and fireplace.

The depot-style main building is where guests check in. It has a book lending library, complimentary snowshoes and is also where the continental breakfast is served each morning. There is a large fire pit outside of the depot and guests can enjoy a campfire with s'mores on Friday and Saturday nights during the summer months. Northern Rail has been in business since 2002 and is open year round.

# Old Jail Bed & Breakfast

349 Government Street
Taylors Falls, MN 55084
651-465-3112
www.theoldjail.com
$$

The Old Jail B & B occupies two adjacent buildings in the middle of Taylors Falls on a hill overlooking the St. Croix River valley. The main building dates to 1851, when it housed the "Cave Saloon". A tunnel connected the saloon to a brewery, and the beer was stored in the tunnel to keep it cool. In 1869, a nearby stable was moved to the site and set atop the saloon, creating today's three-story structure. The jail was built next to the saloon in 1884.

The Old Jail B & B has four guest rooms. One room is located in the old jail, which is entered through the old iron grate jail door. Once inside, little vestige of the jail remains. The ground floor holds a small kitchen, a central potbelly stove and a comfortable living room area. The bedroom is in a large sleeping loft, which holds a full bed.

We stayed in the main building in the "cave", the ground floor that formerly was the saloon. It is called the cave because the first twenty feet of the old tunnel has been incorporated into the guest suite, holding a walk-in shower and an air-jetted tub for two. The suite has a queen bed, a comfortable living room area, a dining room and a kitchen. The rumor is that the suite is haunted, and we did experience some strange happenings with the lights.

Two more guest rooms are located on the second floor. We did not see them, but expect that they are very nice based on the two rooms we did see. Taylors Falls is an active tourist community, with several restaurant choices, a paddle wheel boat tour available, and a riverside park with paths leading to glacial "potholes" and other interesting rock formations.

The Old Jail Bed & Breakfast is open year round.

# Spicer Castle

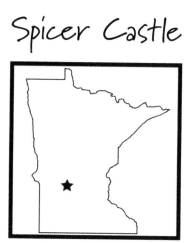

P. O. Box 307
Spicer, MN 56288
800-821-6675   320-796-5870
www.spicercastle.com
$$$

The "castle" and five cottages are set on a bluff on the southeast corner of Green Lake, and have a magnificent view of the lake. John Spicer founded Spicer, Minnesota and was the builder of the property. The main building, a cottage, was built in 1893. It was frequently remodeled and added to until it took its current form in 1913. John Spicer called the place "Medayto Cottage" using the native Dakota Indian name for the lake.

The cottage became a castle when local fishermen began using the cottage as a landmark and referring to it as a castle. It appeared on fishing maps as Spicer's Castle in the 1930's and the name stuck.

The 120-year-old castle is furnished mostly with original furniture, now antiques. The ground floor houses the dining rooms, parlor, reception desk and enclosed porches. The second floor contains six bedrooms, two sleeping porches, and a bathroom for dinner guests. Each bedroom has an antique bed, a private toilet and bath with a tub of some sort, many claw-footed.

Five separate cottages are on the property, and two of the cottages have two bedrooms. We chose to stay in the most rustic cottage, Raymond's Cabin, located on the bluff with a nice lake view. The main floor held a room with a seating area near a large fireplace, a Jacuzzi tub and a dining table at a window facing the lake. A small bathroom had a very small, metal shower. A steep ladder led to the sleeping loft.

In addition to being a B & B, Spicer Castle is a local restaurant that serves dinner seven nights a week. They specialize in game meats cooked over an outdoor grill. On Friday and Saturday nights, the restaurant hosts hilarious "Murder Mystery" dinners.

The Spicer Castle is open year round.

# Whistle Stop B & B

107 E. Nowell Street
New York Mills, MN 56567
800-328-6315   218-385-2223
www.whistlestopbedandbreakfast.com
Jann Lee, Owner
$$ - $$$


Jann Lee moved to New York Mills with her late husband Roger in 1991. They bought a large, three-story home built in 1903 and remodeled it into a B & B decorated on a railroad theme. This is appropriate, as there is a major rail line running through New York Mills and you can hear the trains rumble through every few hours. Since then, three former passenger cars and a caboose have been added to the Whistle Stop and have been beautifully restored.

We stayed in the "Viking Car", elegantly restored in a Victorian motif in 2009. The entire car is one suite. This makes for one huge suite with lots of room for amenities and decorations. From one end to the other, we had available to us the platform as a porch, a dressing table and chair, a queen bed with brass headboard, a dining table, a parlor area with fireplace, a sauna, a kitchenette, and a bath with a whirlpool tub and shower.

The car was decorated in deep purple and green with dark wood panels and a gold ceiling. Many of the windows were colored glass, which provided beautiful lighting inside. The attention to detail in the restoration was apparent.

Breakfast was delivered to the door of our railcar in a large basket, and it was impressive. We were served juice, coffee, fresh blueberry scones, ham and eggs, and a German pancake with fruit inside. In keeping with the elegant décor, fresh flowers accompanied the breakfast.

The Whistle Stop B & B has been in business since 1993 and is open year round.

# The Shack Up Inn

001 Commissary Road
Clarksdale, MS 38614
662-624-8329
www.shackupinn.com
$

The Shack Up Inn got started kind of by accident on the old Hopson Plantation and has grown on the basis of its authenticity, its uniqueness and its ties to Delta Blues music. The plantation's cotton gin is no longer operating, the equipment has been removed, and the space now houses the lobby, a bar, the Juke Joint Chapel and a restaurant. The Juke Joint Chapel contains a stage, and hosts live music on Monday nights, during festivals and on some weekends.

The plantation began growing cotton in 1854. After the Civil War, sharecroppers planted and harvested cotton for plantations and they often lived in shacks located near the fields they tended. In 1944, along with International Harvester, the Hopson Plantation planted and harvested the first mechanical cotton crop. The sharecroppers' livelihood soon disappeared.

In the late 1900's, farmers realized that they were paying taxes on the old sharecropper shacks located on their farms, and began razing them. Hopson owners Guy and Bill decided to preserve some of these shacks by moving them to the gin yard and refurbishing them. Hopson was no longer a working farm, and private individuals owned portions of the old gin yard and its outbuildings. Soon people were asking if they could stay in the shacks or outbuildings overnight and the idea of renting them out was born. Fifteen years later, the Shack Up Inn can uniquely house 100 guests. Trip Advisor has called the Shack Up Inn one of the ten most unique places to stay in the US.

We toured the Robert Clay shack. Mr. Clay raised seven children in this shack with no electricity or running water. His grown children tried to move him to a modern place in his later years, but he refused to go. While Guy and Bill were remodeling the shack, adding modern plumbing, electricity and A/C, they found Robert Clay's moonshine still in the attic. Now we know why he wouldn't move!

We chose to stay in the "Sky Shack", which is inside the cotton gin building and has a proper sittin' porch overlooking the Juke Joint Chapel stage. The décor is deliberately "shacky". We had a wood wall partially made of old doors. Our ceiling was rusted tin roof. But despite the intentional backwoods ambiance, everything was clean, the air conditioning worked well, and we had a comfortable bed and seating. And we enjoyed watching the live music from our porch.

You must be 25 years old or older to rent a room here, but children can stay with adult supervision. The Shack Up Inn is open year round.

# School House Bed & Breakfast

504 3rd Street
Rocheport, MO 65279
573-698-2022
www.schoolhousebb.com
Mike & Lisa Friedemann
$$$ - $$$$

The four-level, brick schoolhouse was built in 1914 and operated as a school until 1972. At one time, it housed grades 1 through 12 in its four, large classrooms. In its final years, it served as a grade school.

One of the large classrooms on the second floor now contains a kitchen and dining area where breakfast is served. Each afternoon, Lisa also bakes up a batch of fresh cookies to welcome guests to the B & B.

Each of the other three classrooms has been remodeled into three guest rooms, each with its own private bath. Our room had a queen bed, two comfortable overstuffed chairs, and a flat screen TV. Several of the rooms have two-person Jacuzzi's in them. Several nice outdoors patios are available for guest use, but we were visiting during a brutal heat wave, so enjoyed the air conditioning.

The Friedemann's were very welcoming and accommodating. We and another couple staying there needed to leave early the next morning. Rather than have us skip breakfast, they accommodated us with an early meal in the "Teachers' Lounge" in the lower level of the building.

We particularly enjoyed dinner in the tiny town of Rocheport. A small place known as the "Rocheport General Store" has live music on weekend nights and serves upscale bar food. It was only a short walk from the schoolhouse, and made for a pleasant evening.

The School House B & B is open year round.

# Treehouse Cabins at River of Life Farms

1746 River of Life Drive
Dora, MO 65637
417-261-7777
www.treehousecabins.com
$$ - $$$$$

The River of Life Farm occupies 350 acres of southern Missouri wilderness, including a full mile of frontage along the North Fork of the White River. This river is considered to be one of the best wild rainbow trout rivers in the Midwest. Activities at the farm include hiking, fishing on your own or with guides, and float trips. The farm is located near Springfield and Branson.

The tree house cabins are large, clean, well-built structures on steel supports. We toured four of the ten tree houses. The newest one, the Lighthouse, sits right on the river and offers a spectacular view looking down the river from a spacious porch.

Each tree house has a different configuration, so you can find accommodations suitable for one couple, two couples, or a family. Lodging is also available in the main lodge, where meals are served and a small store offers sundries and snacks. This would be a great place for either a family reunion or a romantic getaway.

Getting to the farm requires a 2-mile drive down a dirt road, but the directions on the website are easy to follow. Myron and Annie are the owners of the River of Life Farm and they are very personable hosts. The River of Life Farm is open year round.

# 1916 Schoolhouse

416 Cinnabar Basin Road
Gardiner, MT 59030
406-848-7862
http://www.wilderness-connection.com/schoolhouse.html
Rob & Stacy Stermitz
$$$$

The Stermitz Ranch, a working horse and cattle ranch, is located in the mountains near Yellowstone National Park, only 12 miles from the park's north entrance at Gardiner. The Stermitz family has owned the ranch since it was established in 1900. A number of the ranch's historic buildings, including a former school, are being renovated as cabins for anyone to enjoy.

The 1916 Schoolhouse was built in six weeks, cost $400 to build, and was active as a school until 1950. It sits in its original location, on a hill surrounded by meadows and mountains. This one room, rural school was completely renovated in 2010, and charmingly displays many of the original period pieces, including the school desks, a cabinet full of the original schoolbooks, chalkboard and alphabet (Palmer method), potbelly stove, and wood floors. Black and white photographs on the walls are historic and include school children and teachers from years past.

The original library was converted into a bathroom that includes a tiled shower and heated floors. The Schoolhouse also has a kitchen with a full sized range, microwave, apron sink, and an under-counter refrigerator. The main room consists of a king bed, 2 twin pullout mattresses, a seating area with a propane fireplace, and a salvaged wood plank from a local bridge that serves as a dining area. Amazing views are found from every window, and wildlife, such as elk, deer, bears, coyotes, wolves, eagles, hawks, badgers, moose and bison are often seen in the fields nearby.

There are many activities available on the Stermitz Ranch – hiking, horseback riding, zip lining, cross-country skiing and snowshoeing are all located on the property, and whitewater rafting is available on the nearby Yellowstone River.

The Schoolhouse is available for lodging year-round, with a 3-night minimum in the summer. Shorter stays are available in the off-season.

# Izaak Walton Inn

290 Izaak Walton Inn Road
Essex, MT 59916
406-888-5700
www.izaakwaltoninn.com
$$$$

The Great Northern Railroad built the Izaak Walton Inn in 1939 to house their winter workers, who were needed to keep the pass open between Essex and East Glacier, Montana. From the beginning, they made the 29 rooms available to travelers, when rail crew didn't need them. With its railroad history, it is fitting that the inn now offers lodging in eight rail cars, one of them the only one of its kind.

The inn has four regular cabooses. A green and a blue caboose both sleep four people. They have a full bed on the main level and another full bed in the cupola. A red caboose sleeps four with two single beds on the main floor and two single beds in the cupola. An orange caboose has a one full bed and a fireplace. All four cabooses have a kitchenette equipped with a two-burner stove, small fridge, microwave, toaster, coffee maker and an outdoor grill.

The inn also has four luxury rail cars. The Great Northern 441 is the only former diesel locomotive in the United States (perhaps anywhere) that has been remodeled for guest lodging. The locomotive still has its cab intact, so guests can see what a working locomotive looked like. The interior has a 400-year old oak floor and the walls have accents of birch, cedar and cottonwood. There is a stone fireplace and bronze fixtures. The master bedroom has a king bed and there is a queen sleeper sofa. A picture window looks out to the Great Northern rail yard. There is a full kitchen with granite countertops.

The JJ Caboose is named after James Jerome Hill, the man who built the Great Northern Railroad. Its interior is decorated in wood, leather and stone in the same luxurious manner as the locomotive. It has a queen bed in the master bedroom and a full bed in the cupola. There is a full kitchen with granite counter tops.

The Great Northern x215 is a caboose that sleeps four. It has a king bed and fireplace in the master bedroom and is decorated like the JJ Caboose. It features a full kitchen, as well.

The Northern Pacific caboose was formerly a crew car. It can sleep six people. A queen bed and fireplace are in the master bedroom and there are two sets of bunk beds in another room. The Northern Pacific also has a full kitchen.

The Izaak Walton Inn is located just outside of Glacier National Park. It is a cross-country ski resort, has its own restaurant, and is open year round.

# Lodgepole Gallery & Tipi Village

P. O. Box 1832
Hwy 89 Durham Road
Browning, MT 59417
406-338-2787
www.blackfeetculturecamp.com
$

The Lodgepole Gallery and Tipi Village is located on 200 acres of open, high plains, 2 ½ miles west of the town of Browning. The Tipi Village has eleven tipis, from 16 to 20 feet in diameter. The tipis are built in the authentic style of the Blackfeet Indians, and staying in the village provides a glimpse of Blackfeet culture. The Tipi Village is not a B & B, but breakfast and a Blackfeet dinner can be added to your stay. Just outside of the tipi village, a small herd of traditional Blackfeet horses (Spanish Mustangs) graze.

When you arrive, you check in at the art gallery. The dining room is located in this building for breakfast and dinner. A separate building adjacent to the gallery houses modern bath and shower facilities for the tipi guests. The tipis are erected in an area just down the hill from the gallery. They have authentic, double wall construction and have a small fire pit dug into the center of the tipi. You need to bring your own sleeping bag, and you can sleep directly on the ground or rent a pad to put under your bag.

A circular, open roofed shelter is located adjacent to the tipis. It contains picnic tables and a large fire pit. This would be a great gathering place for a large group staying at the tents.

We joined ten other tipi guests for dinner. We were the only people at the village who were not either coming from or going to Glacier National Park. The dinner was served family style with the food set up as a buffet. We ate bison meatloaf, local rainbow and brook trout, chicken, sautéed squash and peppers, homemade bread and a salad.

We did light a small fire in our tipi, as the night was cool even though it was mid-July. The fire took the chill out of the air, but it smoked up the tipi as it died. We left the tipi for a while and were treated to some awesome stargazing. A few moments looking at the stars made the moniker "Big Sky Country" seem just right.

Although modern bath facilities are provided, this stay qualifies as rustic because of sleeping on the ground in your own sleeping bag. Definitely bring a flashlight along, as well. The Tipi Village is open from May through September.

# The Shire of Montana

9 Hobbit Lane
Trout Creek, MT 59874
406-827-7200
www.theshireofmontana.com
Steve & Chris Michaels
$$$$

Hobbits are a fictional humanoid race created by JRR Tolkien. Two hobbits, Bilbo and Frodo Baggins, play key roles in his classic works, "The Hobbit" and "The Lord of the Rings". Hobbits are short, stout and have large, hairy feet for their size. They are fond of a simple life of farming, living comfortably, eating six times a day and socializing. They live in hobbit-holes, which are dug into hills and notable for their round doors and windows.

The Michaels have built a one-of-a-kind hobbit house, and an entire Shire in miniature, on 20 acres of beautiful Montana mountainside. The 1,000 square foot cottage sits amid pine trees on a hill overlooking Whitepine Valley. The dome interior is spacious and very comfortable with a full kitchen, a master bedroom with a king bed, a second bedroom with a single bed, a shared modern bath, and a sitting area. In good hobbit fashion, creature comforts are foremost, including a flat screen TV with a Blu-Ray CD player and XM radio for music.

The 20 acres surrounding the hobbit house are full of whimsical surprises. Look at the base of the trees and you find miniature doors, stairs and other evidence from the fairy and elf kingdoms. There is a fairy village, Bilbo and Frodo Baggin's home, and an artificial stream named the "River Shire", with a bridge. As you cross the bridge, motion activated sensors trigger sounds of trolls or fairies coming from under the bridge. Over 200 crystal dragonflies are scattered throughout the property.

The hobbit house is not a B & B, but there are restaurants within a ten-minute drive. We brought in our dinner with us and cooked it on the propane grill provided on a large deck that overlooks the valley and the Michael's alpaca ranch. While we were cooking, we watched a moose go for a swim in the Michael's pond. Our stay came with a gift basket, including a complimentary bottle of wine and fresh eggs for breakfast from the Michael's well fed hens.

The full magic of The Shire comes to life after dark. All of the miniature hobbit homes, the fairy village, a troll house, the stream and over 200 dragonflies are lighted. In the dark you feel that you are in just one of many inhabited hobbit homes. The solar-powered dragonflies change colors, animating the lighting.

The Huffington Post named The Shire of Montana the "one weirdest, quirkiest thing in the entire state of Montana" in 2014.

The Shire of Montana is open May 1 to November 1 and requires a two-night minimum on weekends and holidays.

# The Convent House
# Bed & Breakfast

311 Hickory
Steinhauer, NE 68441
402-869-2230
www.conventhousebb.com
$

The Convent House is located in the bucolic town of Steinhauer, 85 miles south of Omaha and 65 miles south of Lincoln. The B & B is housed in a former convent and its attached former school. It is a handsome, red brick, two-story structure.

The Convent House has a banquet room in the former school, a garden room, a dining room and a chapel. There are six guest rooms located on three floors of the former convent. A private patio with a waterfall is outside, along with a backyard with a gazebo.

The six guest rooms were each decorated with funds donated by families who are past or present members of Steinauer's St. Anthony's Church. Period furnishings and memorabilia from each family create a unique ambience for each room. The rooms looked cozy and comfortable. The larger basement room offers a more contemporary décor and is ideal for families and hunters.

Steinhauer is a very small town. We did not see any places to shop or eat in town. Slightly larger towns are nearby that can fill those functions with a short drive. The Convent House is available year round.

# Two Rivers Caboose Park

Two Rivers State Recreation Area
27702 F Street
Waterloo, NE 68069
402-359-5165   Res 402-471-1414
www.NGPC.Two.Rivers@nebraska.gov
$

Two Rivers Caboose Park has ten Union Pacific cabooses that have been remodeled as cabins within the Two Rivers Recreation Area. The integrity of the cabooses was retained in the remodeling process. They still have their steel grate platforms and 25" doors.

The interior of the cabooses is done in knotty pine walls and wooden floors. Each caboose is air-conditioned. They sleep six people on four bunk beds at one end of the caboose and two bunks in the center cupola. Under the cupola is a nice sized bath and shower. The other end of the caboose contains a kitchenette with a two-burner stove, a small fridge, a microwave and a sink, a dinette set with four chairs and a couch. Outside, each caboose has a deck with picnic table and charcoal grill. A fire pit is located at ground level.

If you want to stay here, you need to bring some gear. While mattresses are provided, you will need your own bedding or sleeping bags. You also need to bring your own towels and soap, cooking utensils, plates, glasses and silverware. If you want to use the charcoal grill, bring your own charcoal and lighter.

The Two Rivers State Recreation Area encompasses 644 acres of land and 320 acres of water in the form of sand pit lakes along the Platte River. It has a swimming beach, picnicking, fishing (one lake is stocked with trout), playgrounds and a concession stand. Bikes are available for rent, but you need your own helmet.

Caboose rentals are available from May 1 through September 30 each year.

# Adventure Suites

3440 White Mountain Highway
N. Conway, NH 03860
603-356-9744
www.adventuresuites.com
$$ - $$$$

Adventure Suites is an independent motel that had 17 themed rooms available when we stayed there. In 2002, the motel began offering waterbeds and Jacuzzi's in each room. The founder's daughter began remodeling rooms to themes when she took over operations, and the motel continues to evolve. We toured a new "Disco" room that was scheduled to open soon, the 18th room.

Rooms are available in several price ranges. The Economy Suites ($$) include the themes "B & B", "Sugar Shack", "Love Shack", and "Desert Island". The Deluxe Suites ($$$) include "Log Cabin", "Dragon's Lair", "Wine Cellar", and "Victorian Spa". The Super Suites($$$) include "Motorcycle Madness", "NY Penthouse", "Treehouse", "Roman Rendezvous", "Showtime", "The Cave", "The Jungle", and "Owners Quarters". There is one Super Duper Suite ($$$$), "The Club".

The Adventure Suites offers a tour of any unoccupied rooms at 3:00 each afternoon, so we were able to see several rooms. All of the themes were well done. We stayed in the "Love Shack", which had a waterbed with overhead mirrors, a heart-shaped hot tub with mirrors, sexy lighting, bright colors and a great music system.

If you stay here, be sure to come out of your room and go outside behind the motel. You will find outdoor seating looking out at the mountains, a children's playhouse, a very nice fire pit, and grills you can use.

The Adventure Suites is open year round. North Conway has numerous shopping and dining opportunities.

# Caribbean Motel

5600 Ocean Avenue
Wildwood Crest, NJ 08260
609-522-8292
www.caribbeanmotel.com
$ - $$$$

The Caribbean Motel is a lovingly restored, vintage motel that first opened in 1957 with futuristic architecture and exotic, tropical flair. The motel celebrates the Doo Wop music heritage of the Wildwood area. It is on the National Register of Historic Places and is a member of Historic Hotels of America.

One look around and you know you are in a special place. The architecture includes a futuristic "levitating" ramp to the second floor, recessed "spaceship" lights, canted glass walls, and exotic tropical themes, including the first plastic palm trees ever planted in the area. The palm trees surround the C-shaped pool and create the illusion of a tropical paradise.

The entire motel is decorated in bright yellow and greens that look very 1950's. The room doors are bright green. The lounge chairs around the pool are dark green. The rooms have green walls, green rugs, and multi-hued green bed covers. All rooms are equipped with flat screen TV's and refrigerators. Some rooms also have kitchenettes.

The motel is spectacular at night. The pool is lighted and the multi-colored "spaceship" lights stud the walls. The huge, neon "Caribbean Motel" sign casts an eerie blue-green glow on the motel's yellow walls. You feel like you are visiting another world.

What really takes the motel over the top is the Doo Wop music. Sirius Satellite Radio's 1950's channel is playing Doo Wop music throughout the motel. You can hear it in all of the common areas. And you also have a speaker in your room with your own volume control. You can turn it down, or off, or you can crank it up and rock the night away.

The Caribbean Motel, a serious feel-good place, is open year round. Oh, and by the way, the Atlantic Ocean is only one block away.

# Blue Swallow Motel

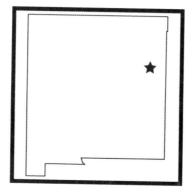

815 E. Route 66 Blvd
Tucumcari, NM 88401
575-461-9849
www.blueswallowmotel.com
Kevin & Nancy Mueller

The Blue Swallow Motel is the oldest continually operating motel in Tucumcari, and has been a fixture on historic Route 66 for decades. The Blue Swallow began in 1939 and most likely welcomed its first guests in 1941. It was originally constructed with twelve rooms in six cabins, but the cabins were soon joined together with garages for guests' cars. A number of those garages have murals on their interior walls today.

The Blue Swallow is easy to find. Its large, blue, neon sign sits along Route 66 with a Model A Ford parked under the sign. The office and owners' quarters are adjacent to the sign in a building that was a café during the heyday of the motel and Route 66. Miss Lillian Redmond owned the motel for 40 years. Tucumcari is the largest city between Abilene and Albuquerque, making Tucumcari a natural stop, and Miss Lillian made the Blue Swallow a fixture of the highway.

The Pixar movie "Cars" celebrates Route 66 culture. In that movie, the "Cozy Cone Motel", is a combination of the Blue Swallow Inn, the Wigwam Motel (California), and Ray's Café.

When Interstate 40 opened in the 1960's, businesses in Tucumcari were hit hard. The town is still not prospering, but there are 25 huge murals located in the town to see, museums to tour, restaurants and shops to visit, as well as tons of history to explore.

The Muellers bought the Blue Swallow in 2011 and have revitalized it. All of the neon signs have been restored to their heyday glory. At night the huge blue road sign, red and yellow neon in the parking lot and small neon blue swallows along the exterior walls, light the entire premises. Room décor celebrates the 1940's era and Route 66.

In early evening as the setting sun shaded the motel exterior, some of the guests began to pull the lawn chairs outside their door into a circle in the shade. Kevin and Nancy joined their guests for an impromptu cocktail hour. Before long, almost all the guests had joined in and were sharing stories. Most of the group headed to a local restaurant afterwards. The gathering was a relaxing way to end a day on the road and left us with a lasting affection for the Blue Swallow Motel.

The Blue Swallow is open year round.

# Heliohouse Earthship

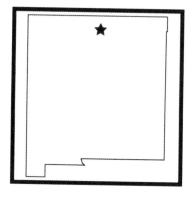

Hwy 64 W
El Prado (Taos), NM
866-343-4171
www.heliohouse.com
Michael & Jill Lickley, Hosts
$$$

Heliohouse offers a chance to live "off the grid" in great comfort. The Greater World Earthship Community is located on the 7,000-foot elevation Taos Mesa, 15 minutes by car northwest of Taos. It is on the north side of Hwy 64 about two miles west of the Rio Grande Gorge Bridge. The community describes itself as "a sustainable subdivision comprising 650 acres of rolling mesa with broad views of the Sangre de Cristo Mountains".

So what is an "earthship"? Earthships are constructed of natural and recycled materials, utilize solar and thermal heating and cooling, derive electric power solely from their own solar cells and wind generators, harvest their own water and treat their own sewage. They have no connections to any utilities, are self-sustaining, and thus "off the grid".

Heliohouse is a one bedroom, one bath, earthship rental. The house is dug into the earth on three sides and faces south. The south side is composed of almost floor to ceiling windows. A three-foot wide strip of plant bedding runs the length of the house just inside the windows. The beds were growing with decorative plants because Heliohouse is a rental, but could sustain herbs and vegetables as a home. The interior is decorated in attractive, earth tone tiles throughout. The ceilings are made of knotty pine and the walls are a mixture of stucco, tile and pine.

Heliohouse is furnished very comfortably. The great room has a sofa, recliner, tables and a wood stove for heat. The kitchen has a refrigerator and freezer, a propane stove, dishes, cooking utensils and a stock of coffee, tea and sundries. You do need to bring your own food, unless you head to Taos for meals. The bedroom has a queen bed, dresser and TV. The bath has a claw-footed tub and shower hose.

Staying in an earthship is a bit like living on a boat, in that you need to be aware of your use of resources. Heliohouse is a great place to stay to explore Taos, while having a peaceful respite to return to at night. And at 7,000 feet, the night sky is an awesome sight.

Heliohouse is open year round and has a two-night minimum. Michael and Jill are friendly hosts who will teach you how to live "off the grid".

# Kokopelli Cave Bed & Breakfast

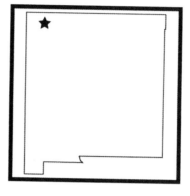

5001 Antelope Junction
Farmington, NM 87402
505-860-3812
www.kokocave.com
Gayle Davis, Manager

Kokopelli Cave provides the unique opportunity to spend the night in great comfort 70-feet underground, while still having magnificent sunset views from 230-feet up looking over the La Plata River Valley. Say what?

The Kokopelli Cave was blasted out of a 300-foot bluff in 1981. It was originally intended as a geologist's office, which proved to be impractical. So in 1997, the cave became a B & B. The cave is large, 1,700 square feet, and has two glass door entrances and outdoor seating areas. The cave is reached by descending seventy feet from the top of the bluff along a steep path with steps cut into the sandstone.

The bedroom is furnished with a queen bed, dresser and stereo system. A central sandstone pillar separates a living room with two couches and flat screen TV, a replica Native American kiva, and a fully equipped kitchen. The entire cave except the bath and a portion of the kitchen is carpeted. The large bath is carved in a separate niche and has a stone Jacuzzi and waterfall shower. The cave has electric and modern plumbing. No air conditioning is needed because the cave temperature naturally stays below 73° year round. A space heater is provided for cooler weather.

The address above is where we met Gayle Davis, the manager. We had stopped before meeting her to buy our evening's dinner to take with us. The climb down to the cave entrance was not strenuous, but not something we wanted to tackle after dark, returning from dinner. Gayle led us to the cave and showed us around, and provided us with a continental breakfast before departing.

Numerous "critters" visit the cave entrance and there is a supply of cat food and birdseed available for feeding them on the porch, if you choose to do so. We watched squirrels and chipmunks feed, and saw a hawk trying to feed on them. Ring-tailed cats frequently visit the cave entrance, but we were not fortunate enough to see them. In the morning, it was very cool to have numerous hummingbirds surround us as we enjoyed our morning coffee out on the rock patio.

The walls of the cave are sandstone. Some guests have begun a tradition of leaving small gifts and unusual rocks in the nooks and crannies of the walls. We wished that we had known that in advance. We would have brought a small seashell from our Florida home.

The Kokopelli Cave is open from March to the end of November. No pets are allowed and the cave is non-smoking.

# Caboose Motel

60483 State Route 415
Avoca, NY 14809
607-566-2216
Patricia Thomas, Owner
$

The Caboose Motel consists of five cabooses and a small motel located in upstate New York, only a mile from I-390 just north of its intersection with I-86. All five cabooses are painted red and have center cupolas. They differ in appearance by carrying the logo of different historic railroads. Several railroad crossing signs and an old Railway Express luggage wagon decorate the grounds.

Each caboose can sleep five people. At one end there is a double and a single bed. There are two more single beds in each side of the cupola. This layout is ideal for a couple with children. The cabooses also have a small table and two chairs, a TV, a coffee maker, a bathroom and shower. Three of the cabooses have a small fridge and a microwave, as well. Outside there are chairs, a picnic table, grills and a fire pit.

The cabooses are not fancy, but have an authentic feel. The interior is a mix of painted metal panels and wood panels. Our caboose was basic, but clean and comfortable.

The town of Avoca does not have much dining available, but Bath is only five miles away, and it has both local restaurants and fast food available. The Glenn Curtiss Museum is located in nearby Hammondsport and it is worth a visit. About half the museum is devoted to the pioneer aviation achievements of Curtiss, and the other half has an eclectic collection of all things old.

The Caboose Motel is very child friendly. It has been in business since 1986. The motel is open year-round and the cabooses are open from April through October, weather permitting.

# Kate's Lazy Meadow

5191 Rt. 28
Mt Tremper, NY 12457
845-688-7200
www.lazymeadow.com
$$$$

Kate's Lazy Meadow is located in the Catskill Mountains about ten miles from Woodstock. The property consists of nine acres of meadow along Esopus Creek. It is truly a beautiful setting.

Lazy Meadow has six suites at the main site, and three separate cabins nearby. We stayed in the Sacajawea suite, which was decorated with southwest prints and pictures of Native-American women. The suite was very comfortable with a queen bed, fireplace, small kitchenette, TV and DVD. Our suite shared a large porch with the other suite in the building, and the porch looked toward Esopus Creek.

The other suites were done in a bold color palette and decorated in a 1950's style. The kitchens, in particular, are very retro. At one time, there were a number of Airstream travel trailers on the property near the creek. These have now been moved to the high desert of California. (See Kate's Lazy Desert, California.)

Kate is Kate Pierson, lead singer of the B-52s. Look closely at some of the items in the suites. Many of the toiletries are from places she stayed while on the road touring. And some of the items in the suites represent shopping sprees while touring, as well

Kate's Lazy Meadow is open year round.

# Saugerties Lighthouse

168 Lighthouse Drive
Saugerties, NY 12477
845-247-0656
www.saugertieslighthouse.com
$$$$

A lighthouse has operated at the junction of Esopus Creek and the Hudson River since 1835. The current Saugerties Lighthouse was built in 1869, and is still operational. To reach the lighthouse, you need to walk about a half-mile along a boggy path. The Hudson River is tidal and you should check the tide tables before making the trek, as parts of the path can be under water at peak high tides.

The lighthouse has two bedrooms on the second floor. Both have views of the river. Each bedroom has a double bed and is heated by a coal stove in the winter. There is no air conditioning, but cooling breezes are available most of the time because of the location of the lighthouse on the river.

The two bedrooms share a single bathroom that is located on the ground floor with the kitchen and a parlor. The bathroom has a basin, a shower, and a composting toilet. A large coal stove heats the comfortable parlor.

A hearty breakfast is included with your stay. You can bring food to the lighthouse to cook on the stove or an outdoor propane grill. You can also walk into the town of Saugerties to dine, tides permitting. A large picnic area is located on the river side of the lighthouse.

The Saugerties Lighthouse is open year round from Thursday through Sunday. A two-night minimum stay is required on weekends.

# Tibbetts Point Lighthouse Hostel

33439 County Road 6
Cape Vincent, NY 13618
315-654-3450
www.capevincent.org/lighthouse
$

The Tibbetts Point Lighthouse is located on the south shore of Lake Ontario at the point where the outflow of water forms the St. Lawrence River. A lighthouse was first built here in 1827, and the current structure dates from 1854. The Fresnel lens that was installed in 1854 is the only original Fresnel lens that is still operating on Lake Ontario. The light was automated in 1981.

The keeper's quarters were turned into a youth hostel in 1984. The hostel has three rooms with two beds, one room with four beds, and two rooms with six beds. Groups and singles are welcome. The hostel does not provide any meals, but a self-catering kitchen is available for guests to use. The town of Cape Vincent is 2.5 miles from the lighthouse.

The hostel is open from July 1 through September 7 each year.

Red Caboose Getaway Inn, WA

Featherbed Railroad caboose interior, CA

# Castle McKenzie at Tulach Ard

1517 Moccasin Creek Road
Murphy, NC
828-557-1999
www.castlemckenzie.com
$$$

Tulach ard means High hill in Gaelic, and Castle McKenzie does indeed command a high hill in the beautiful Smoky Mountains. The castle is the size of a home now, but plans are to continue building onto the structure to make it a larger castle in the future.

When we visited, the upper level of the castle was available to rent. The rental includes two bedrooms, two full baths, a complete kitchen, dining area and living room. The master bedroom has a king bed and its own Jacuzzi tub. The second bedroom has a queen bed. The interior features ten-foot ceilings, extensive stonework and copper fixtures.

The living room has a large fireplace and a flat screen TV. Both bedrooms access the upstairs porch that faces down the hill and overlooks a pond, dubbed "Braveheart Pond". A six-person hot tub is located in a castle turret outside of the master bedroom.

The lower level was under construction when we visited and was not part of the rental. Plans are to finish the lower level with a home theater, recreation room, den, Scottish pub and a "dungeon" bedroom.

Castle McKenzie requires a two-night minimum and is open year round.

# Falling Waters Adventure Resort

10345 US Highway 74 West
Bryson City, NC 28713
800-451-9972
www.fallingwatersresort.com
$

Wildwater, Ltd., has been offering white water rafting experiences in the mountains of North Carolina since 1971. Currently they offer whitewater rafting, float trips, jeep tours, zip lining, and railroad adventures from five locations. At two locations they offer yurt lodging. Wildwater offers group lodging in five yurts that can accommodate up to 34 people at their Chatooga Center location. We stayed in one of their yurts at their Falling Waters Resort.

Falling Waters has eight yurts located in a wooded setting off Highway 74 southwest of Bryson City. Six of the yurts form a circle around a central bathhouse. Two of the yurts are nearby on a spur overlooking a lake and waterfall. All eight sleep two persons each.

Each yurt is set on a wooden platform that includes a nice sized porch. The yurts have a queen bed, a futon, a mini-fridge and a coffee maker. There is no air conditioning, but the shady, wooded setting kept the yurts comfortable even during the day.

The common bathhouse contains four lockable, clean restrooms with showers. Towels are included with the linens provided in your yurt. There is one additional bathroom without a shower. A large hot tub is located on the porch of the bathhouse.

We found the yurts to be comfortable and the setting to be enjoyable. We had one of the yurts on the spur and could see the lake from our porch. The pastoral setting in the woods was quiet and restful. Bryson City is a short drive away and offers several restaurant choices.

Falling Waters' yurts are available from mid-March through November each year.

# The Golden Lamb

27 S. Broadway
Lebanon, OH 45036
513-932-506
www.goldenlamb.com
$$

The Golden Lamb is the oldest continuously operating inn in Ohio. Its license was issued on December 3, 1803 to Jonas Seaman. The current building was built in 1815 with two stories. The third and fourth floors were added in 1878. The inn has 18 guest rooms and each of the rooms is named after a famous person who has stayed at the inn, and there are many. Twelve United States Presidents have stayed at the Golden Lamb, from John Quincy Adams to George W. Bush.

We stayed in the Charles Dickens room. He was a guest at the inn in 1842 when he was 30 years old and touring the US to promote his books. We were welcomed to our room with a letter from the manager that gave a brief history of the room and Mr. Dickens' stay. The room was furnished in antiques, including period chairs, a large bureau with a mirror, and a marble topped dresser with a washbasin. We had a small, but adequate, private bathroom.

The most interesting furniture item in our room was the bed. About 1845, Crawford Riddell of Philadelphia made two beds with enormous headboards. One of those beds resides at the White House in the Lincoln Bedroom, the other was ours for the night.

The Golden Lamb has a Shaker furniture museum on its fourth floor. You are also welcome to look into any of the other guest rooms with open doors.

The Golden Lamb restaurant is a well-regarded dining destination. The Black Horse Tavern is also on premises. The Golden Lamb is open year round.

# Greatstone Castle

429 N. Ohio Avenue
Sidney, OH 45365
937-498-4728
www.greatstonecastle.com
$$

Greatstone Castle sits atop a hill that is just two blocks from the courthouse square of Sidney. It is only a couple of miles east of I-75 via exit 92.

William Henry Collier Goode built the castle over three years between 1892 and 1895. Mr. Goode named the home Whitby Place after his ancestral home in Whitby, England. The family occupied the home for 81 years. The castle is listed on the National Register of Historic Places as the Whitby Mansion.

In 1990, the current owners renamed the property Greatstone Castle and opened it as a B & B. The castle is approximately 17,000 square feet. It endured two major fires in its history. After the second fire, the roof was lowered by nine feet and one floor was eliminated. The now two-story structure has four guest rooms.

We stayed in the master bedroom, which was large, had a working gas fireplace, and was furnished with antiques and a huge four-poster bed. The other guest rooms were furnished similarly.

Each room contains a guidebook for a walking tour of the castle. The walking tour is very well done and worthwhile. While staying there, you are welcome to spend time in any of the many rooms where the doors are open. The castle has beautiful old woodwork, many decorative ceramic tiles and antiques.

The friendly staff offers you a choice of a fruit and cereal breakfast or eggs and toast. The breakfast is served at a time of your choosing. There are several restaurants within a three or four block walking distance of the castle for dinner.

The Greatstone Castle is open year round.

# Nomad Ridge at The Wilds

14000 International Road
Cumberland, OH 43732
740-638-5030
www.thewilds.org
$$$$$

The Wilds is a private, non-profit safari park and conservation center whose mission is to advance conservation through science, education and personal experience. It is built on 9,154 acres of reclaimed strip mine land donated by the American Electric Power Company. Started in 1984, it now houses 31 rare and endangered species, including Sichuan takin, Grevy's zebra, cheetah, giraffe, southern white rhinoceros, African and Asian wild dogs and more.

The Wilds offers safari tours in both air-conditioned and open-air buses. Premium safaris are available in open pickup trucks that can go off-road and approach the animals close up. Also available is zip-lining through the park, sunset safaris, horseback safaris, a wild animal encounter for children and a fishing safari.

Nomad Ridge is located on a ridge overlooking a lake and fenced pasture that holds Pere David deer and Sichuan takin. The ridge has twelve luxury yurts, each set up for two people. Seven of the yurts have queen beds, two have two single beds, and three have king beds. All have bamboo floors and private bathrooms with showers. Most of the yurts have air-conditioning. The yurts are beautifully decorated and were the nicest yurts we stayed in on our trip.

A stay in a yurt at The Wilds includes a safari bus tour, dinner and breakfast. The meals are served in the main lodge after the park closes and before it opens for visitors the next morning. The meals were quite good. Yurt stays are restricted to those over 21 years of age because beer and wine are available for dinner. There are some camping possibilities for children and group stays are available at a private lodge.

Overnight guests can use a large deck with a propane fire pit at its center. We found ourselves mingling at the fire pit with other guests in the evening listening to the bellowing of the Pere David deer and watching the antics of the unusual Sichuan takin below.

The yurts at Nomad Ridge are available seven days a week from May through October. The lodge is open year round.

# Ravenwood Castle

65666 Bethel Road
New Plymouth, OH 45654
740-596-2606
www.ravenwoodcastle.com
$ - $$$$

Ravenwood Castle sits on 50 acres, atop a hill in the Hocking Hills area of southeast Ohio. The castle is based on the design of castles that were built to guard the border between England and Wales during the 12th and 13th centuries. The property consists of the Castle with seven guest rooms, seven cottages in a Medieval Village, five cabins in the Huntsman's Hollow, and two Gypsy Wagons in the nearby woods.

The main castle was completed in 1995, the village cottages opened in 1997, and the Huntsman's Hollow cabins opened in 2014. Long-time Anglophiles Sue and Jim Maxwell built the castle. The Maxwell's took great effort to give the properties a true English feel. Jim and Pam Reed, who enjoyed the castle as guests over the years, purchased Ravenwood in 2012.

Ravenwood Castle's seven guest rooms are all quite large and luxuriously appointed. The rooms have sitting areas, fireplaces and private baths. The seven cottages in the village are decorated to depict the skill of a village artisan, such as a woodcutter, or clock maker. Each has a sitting room and a TV with a DVD player. Several have Jacuzzi tubs. All have porches looking into the woods. Six of the cottages house two guests and the Silversmith cottage can house four. The two Gypsy Wagons offer a more camping-like experience and have a separate bath building. The cabins in the Huntsman's Hollow can sleep from four to six guests.

The castle has a pub that serves handcrafted beers, wines, ciders and mixed drinks, except for Sunday. The castle's library holds books, games and DVD's for guest use. The great dining hall is used for many special events such as murder mysteries and beer tastings. An English garden is located behind the castle. There are walking trails through the 50-acre property.

Breakfast is included with a stay at Ravenwood, and ours was hearty and delicious. Breakfast is served between 8:30 and 10:00 each morning. The pub is open seven days a week serving pub style food for both lunch and dinner (no alcohol on Sunday). A buffet dinner is available most Friday and Saturday nights in the Great Hall. Several restaurants are also available within about a fifteen-minute drive.

Ravenwood requires a two night minimum stay on weekends and during the peak fall foliage season. It is open year round, except for the Gypsy Wagons, which close in the coldest months.

# Abbey Road Farm B & B

10501 NE Abbey Road
Carlton, OR 97111
503-852-6278
www.abbeyroadfarm.com
John & Judi Stuart
$$$ - $$$$

John and Judi Stuart have built a unique, silo-suite B & B on their 82-acre working farm. The B & B is located about 35 miles southwest of Portland in the Willamette Valley near Carlton. The farm sits on a hill looking east at the Guadalupe vineyard and the pine forest of a 1,600-acre Trappist Monastery. Other vineyards are close by for touring.

The B & B is built inside three repurposed Butler corrugated metal grain silos. While the exteriors look like regular grain silos, the interiors have been crafted to resort level standards. A tool shed originally connected the silos, but nowadays a lobby has replaced the tool shed and provides an entryway to the inn's five suites and a common den. A magnificent Murano hand blown glass chandelier in the lobby casts a welcoming pink light in the evening.

King beds are in four of the rooms and a queen bed is in the fifth. All of the rooms have private baths with amenities like towel warmers, a Jacuzzi tub and a separate shower. The rooms have eastern views of the farm and surrounding vineyards. The interiors are so well done that, other than rounded walls, there is little evidence of the grain silo nature of the structure evident from inside.

The Stuarts have created an enjoyable walking tour of their working farm. You can wander at your leisure seeing their English garden, vegetable garden, events facility converted from a horse barn, berry patch, chicken coop, goat pens and 7-acre conservation area with alpacas, sheep, geese and a llama. As you walk, you will enjoy music. Outdoor speakers cover the property and music plays softly in the background from sunup to sundown.

A hearty and healthy breakfast is served at a central kitchen/ dining space, typically featuring eggs and vegetables that come from the farm. A chicken-apple sausage that is made for the inn accompanied our breakfast. For early risers, coffee is available anytime in the lobby via a Keurig coffee maker.

Abbey Road Farm is open year round and requires a two-night stay on weekends and during the high season from June through October.

# Five Mile Butte Lookout Tower

Barlow Ranger District
Mt Hood National Forest
780 NE Court
Dufur, OR 97021
541-467-2291
www.recreation.gov
$

Staying at the Five Mile Butte Lookout Tower is a rugged and rustic camping type experience. Getting to the tower requires a three-mile hike over moderate terrain that typically takes three to four hours. You need to carry in all of your food, water, bedding and toiletries. And you need to carry out all of your garbage.

The tower was built in 1957, is thirty feet tall, and has a 14' by 14' room at the top that is surrounded by a wooden catwalk. It is furnished with a small bed, a wood stove for heating, and a table and chairs. It has a propane cook stove and solar powered lights. There is no water source on site. An outhouse with a vault toilet is provided. The tower is equipped with basic dishes and cooking utensils. Propane and firewood are provided.

The tower sits at an elevation of 4,627 feet atop Five Mile Butte. A forest of ponderosa pine, Douglas fir and western hemlock surrounds it. Wildlife frequenting the area includes turkeys, grouse, deer, elk, coyotes, cougars and bear.

The tower is available from May through November.

# Green Ridge Lookout Tower

P. O. Box 249
Sisters, OR 97759
541-549-7700
$

The Green Ridge Lookout Tower is located on the side of Green Ridge, more than 2,000 feet above the Metolius River in Deschutes National Forest. The lookout room is on a 20-foot tower with views of Mt Jefferson and the Metolius River basin. The tower was built in the 1960's.

There is a parking area at the tower. A short boardwalk leads to a wooden observation deck on the tower. A stairway leads up one flight to the catwalk surrounding the cabin. The one-room cabin is equipped with a futon, a table and two chairs, a propane refrigerator, a propane wall heater, three-burner propane stove and oven, and an overhead light. Basic cooking utensils are also provided.

Guests need to bring their own food, water, bedding and toiletries, including toilet paper. Guests need to remove their trash.

Although one overhead light is provided, additional light sources are recommended.

Green Ridge Lookout is available from mid-May through June, and mid-September through mid-November. Forest Service volunteers staff the lookout during July through mid-September to aid in forest fire detection.

# Heceta Head Light Station

92072 Hwy 101 South
Yachats, OR 97498
866-547-3696   541-547-3696
www.hecetalighthouse.com
$$ - $$$$$

The Heceta Head Light Station is well known for its seven course gourmet breakfasts and for being the most photographed lighthouse on the Pacific coast. The lighthouse sits 205 feet above the Pacific Ocean on a cliff. The Keepers' House is nearby and is 100 feet above the ocean. The setting is spectacular.

The Heceta Head Lighthouse was completed in 1894. It boasts having a huge 1st Order Fresnel lens that was manufactured in England. The light was automated in 1963 and is still active. The light signal is visible 21 miles out to sea. Tours of the lighthouse are available.

The Keepers' House sits inside a one acre fenced yard. It has six guest rooms and five baths. A porch runs the length of the house facing the ocean and has unimpeded views. Inside the house on the ground floor are two parlors with fireplaces, a dining room and two kitchens, one for guests and one for the staff to prepare breakfast. Bedrooms are upstairs. Trails run both uphill from the Keepers' House to the light and down to the beach.

Mike and Carole Korgan, both accomplished chefs, started the B&B in 1995. They decided to make a leisurely, seven-course gourmet breakfast a feature of a stay at the light station. Their daughter Michelle Korgan and chef Steven Bursey operate the B&B today, and they are continuing the tradition.

During our stay, all twelve guests gathered in the dining room at 8:30 for breakfast. Each course was deliberately staged to allow plenty of time for relaxed conversation and enjoyment of the meal. Our breakfast included (1) a fruit cup with mascarpone, (2) freshly baked orange bread, (3) mini bagels served with topping choices of salmon, hazelnut chocolate or jam, (4) a raspberry and white chocolate fruit frappe, (5) a quiche served with pork and potato sausages, (6) a peach coffee cake, and (7) a fruit and cheese plate. Breakfast finishes at about ten o'clock.

Coffee was available before breakfast, so we took ours outside and walked to the edge of the cliff to look at the ocean. We were rewarded by being able to watch otters playing in the kelp along the shore.

The Heceta Head Light Station is open year round.

# McMenamin's Kennedy School

5736 N. E. 33rd Avenue
Portland, OR 97211
888-249-3983   503-249-3983
www.mcmenamins.com
$$

The Kennedy Elementary School opened in 1915 at what was, at that time, the edge of Portland. For 60 years, the school educated thousands of Portland's children from the Concordia neighborhood. The school closed at the end of the 1974-1975 school year due to declining enrollment.

McMenamin's opened the former school as a unique hotel in 1997. They remodeled the classrooms into 57 guest rooms, each with a private bath. It is likely that a walk through the memorabilia packed hallways will bring back memories of a similar school from your past.

The amenities available to you at the Kennedy School will make it unlike any school you ever attended. The former auditorium is now a movie theater showing second run movies, which are complimentary for overnight guests. The movie snack bar includes pub style food, beer and wine that can be delivered to your seat.

McMenamin's operates a craft brewery on the school site and owns both a vineyard and distillery off site. The wares of the brewery, vineyard and distillery can be enjoyed in the Courtyard Restaurant (the former cafeteria), the Honors Bar and Detention Bar (both adults only), the Cypress Room with indoor or outdoor seating (children welcome until 10PM), and the Boiler Room Bar located in the former boiler room and featuring pool tables, shuffleboard and sports bar TV's.

One of the more relaxing venues at the Kennedy School is the soaking pool. The ceramic tiled pool is set in a small courtyard that was formerly the teachers' lounge. The saltwater pool, which is surrounded by gardens, is maintained at 100°. The pool is large enough to accommodate several dozen guests comfortably.

McMenamin's Kennedy School is open year round.

# McMenamin's
# Old St. Francis School

700 N. W. Bond Street
Bend, OR 97701
877-661-4228   541-382-5174
www.mcmenamins.com
$$ - $$$

The St. Francis School opened in 1936 as the first parochial school in central Oregon. In its first year the school served 145 students in grades 1 through 8 in only four classrooms. Classroom additions were made to the school in 1953 and 1960, and in 1968 the school expanded to include a gymnasium, stage, meeting rooms and cafeteria. The school closed in 2000 when a more modern campus was built.

The Old St. Francis School is now a small hotel with 19 guest rooms with king or queen size beds, TV's, complimentary Wi-Fi Internet, and private baths with showers. Overnight stays include complimentary use of the soaking pool and admission to the movie theater. In addition to the classroom lodging, the property has four bungalow-style cottages that sleep from two to ten people.

Guests have a number of dining venues available on site. The Old St. Francis Pub offers breakfast, lunch and dinner. The Fireside Bar has a fireplace and two pool tables. O'Kanes Pub is a quaint bar located in a separate building at the back of the property. The Old St. Francis Brewery is located in the former lunch and music rooms.

The school's former gymnasium has been transformed into a movie theater showing second run movies. Seating is in overstuffed, living room style chairs. The Theater Bar will deliver a pizza or calzone to your seats.

The Old St. Francis Soaking Pool offers a soothing experience. The mosaic-tiled pool features Persian lanterns and an open-air view of the sky. The saltwater pool is heated to 100° and is open until midnight.

The Old St. Francis School is open year round.

# Out N' About Treehouse

300 Page Creek Road
Cave Junction, OR 97523
541-592-2208
www.treehouses.com
$$ - $$$$$

Out N' About may be the mother lode of tree houses in the United States. The tree houses are located on 36 acres of land in southwestern Oregon near the California border. There are numerous tree houses and multiple activities available on the site.

There are 15 tree houses available to guests. Seven of the tree houses are quoted for rent by two people, and eight tree houses by four people. Most of these structures can sleep a few more people, especially if they are children, for a modest bump in the price. Five of the rentals have a full bath, two more have a toilet and sink, and a central bathhouse serves the remaining units. Several of the rentals are part of the main lodge; others are located pretty high up in the trees and are reached by catwalks.

Out N' About is very child friendly and offers many activities. Hiking and biking trails can be accessed directly from the tree houses. Out N' About offers horseback riding, river rafting on either the Klamath or Rouge River, zip-lining on two separate routes, a rock wall, and a 50-foot Tarzan Swing. A fresh water swimming pool is available to guests as well.

Out N' About is a bed and breakfast with a full meal provided to all guests. For other meals there is a designated cooking area with BBQ grills, microwaves and stovetop cookers. The nearest restaurants are located in Cave Junction, a 15-minute drive away.

Bed and bath linens are provided. Guests are advised to bring their own swimming towels and flashlights for getting around after dark.

From Memorial Day through Labor Day minimum stays are required. The choices are to stay Monday-Tuesday, Wednesday-Thursday, or Friday-Saturday-Sunday.

# Cove Haven
# Entertainment Resort

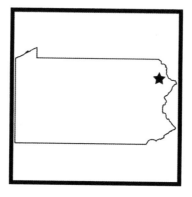

194 Lakeview Drive
Lakeville, PA 18438
800-233-4141   570-226-4506
www.covepoconoresorts.com
$$$ - $$$$$

Cove Haven operates three luxury, romance-themed, resorts in the Pocono Mountains. We could describe the experience as being on a cruise ship, but without the ship. The multi-acre, and multi-building, resort offers a large array of activities, most included with your stay. Activities include archery, a driving range, tennis, basketball, biking, boat rentals and fishing. Indoor activities include bingo, trivia contests, ping-pong, arcades, air hockey, WII bowling and more.

The property has a number of indoor and outdoor pools, a sauna and hot tubs. There are also bars, a café and a gift shop.

Filling out the cruise ship analogy, your breakfast and dinner are included, you prepay gratuities at check-in, and you will be seated at tables of eight for dining. (You can request tables for two, as a few are available.) Nightclub entertainment is available in the evening. The night we were there, music started at 9:00, followed by a rather ribald "Not So Newlywed Game" with audience volunteers.

As for being romance-themed, the whole place is about love, physically expressed. The rooms are large and well sound-proofed, they have circular beds with mirrored headboards, heart-shaped Jacuzzi's for two, lots of mirrors everywhere, subdued lighting, good quality sheets — get the picture?

Cove Haven is open year round. It has two sister properties, Paradise Stream and Pocono Palace, nearby.

# The Red Caboose
# Motel & Restaurant

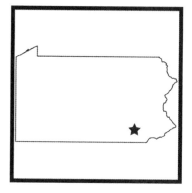

312 Paradise Lane
Ronks, PA 17572
888-687-5005   717-687-5000
www.redcaboosemotel.com
$ - $$$

The Red Caboose Motel is the mother lode of caboose lodging in the United States. The property boasts 38 cabooses, two baggage cars and a restaurant in two restored dining cars. The motel is located in the heart of Amish country in Lancaster County, Pennsylvania. It is a half-mile away from the Strasburg Steam Rail Road and the State Railroad Museum, and across the parking lot from the National Toy Train Museum. The gift shop at the motel is also full of train memorabilia.

Family cabooses have either two double beds, or one double bed at one end and four single bunk beds at the other. Cabooses for two have a sitting area in place of the bunk beds. All cabooses have air-conditioning, bath and shower, microwave, small fridge and flat screen TV with cable. These cabooses are not the most fancy ones you can find, but they are clean, well equipped and a great family venue.

You could stay for multiple days here and not run out of things to do. You can ride the Strasburg Steam Train, take a ride in an Amish buggy, and spend some time in the motel's farm animal petting zoo. On Friday and Saturday night in summer, weather permitting, you can watch a movie projected onto the side of the motel's barn. You can climb to the top of the farm's old silo to a viewing platform. And you can visit the National Toy Train Museum next door.

The Red Caboose Motel owes its start to a dare. A friend dared Don Denlinger to bid on 19 cabooses up for auction in 1969. He put in a ridiculously low bid and forgot about it. Six months later, as the winning bidder, he was scrambling to figure out what to do with them. He moved them to the farm, started remodeling them, and built a motel.

The Red Caboose Motel has been in business since 1970 and is open from March through mid-December each year.

# Rose Island Lighthouse Foundation

P. O. Box 1419
Newport, RI 02840-0997
401-847-4242
www.roseislandlighthouse.org
$$$

The Rose Island Lighthouse is located in the southern part of Narragansett Bay, just west of Newport. It was first lit in 1870 to serve as a link in a chain of navigation aids along the New England Coast. The lighthouse was abandoned in 1970 when the Newport Bridge was built and became a more prominent navigation aid. The lighthouse was restored in 1993 after almost being lost to vandalism and neglect. It is listed on the National Register of Historic Places.

The Lighthouse has two guest bedrooms and a children's sleeping loft available for rent. The Jamestown-Newport Ferry provides access to the island. A stay at the lighthouse is a bit rustic and you need to be in good enough physical condition to climb a 300-foot hill to the lighthouse, as well as get on and off of the boat. You need to bring a cooler (not Styrofoam) with food for your dinner and breakfast. Also keep in mind that weather conditions could require staying an extra day, so prepare accordingly.

The lighthouse and keepers' quarters have been restored to what it looked like circa 1912. From 10:00AM until 4:00PM the site is a museum that is toured by day visitors. When the museum closes, the two bedrooms are turned over to the overnight guests. Guests are considered "guest keepers" and are responsible for changing their own beds and putting the rooms back in order before 10:00. Linens and cleaning supplies are provided.

One shared bathroom is located indoors, but most of the time guests use outdoor, low flow toilets. Washbasins and pitchers are provided indoors, and solar showers are available outdoors. The lighthouse has basic cooking utensils. Cooking is accomplished using a single burner propane stovetop and propane BBQ grill outside.

Lighthouse stays are available from June through October. For those interested in a longer stay, a weeklong keepers program is available using the keeper's apartment on the second floor of the house. As a keeper with real duties, the cost of your stay becomes a tax-deductible donation.

# Tiverton Four Corners School No. 1

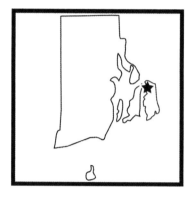

4042 Main Road
Tiverton, RI 02878
401-624-4004
www.sakonnetfarm.com
$$$ - $$$$

The Tiverton Four Corners School building was originally constructed in 1800 by one of the pioneer families in the area. In 1854, it was turned over to the town as a one-room schoolhouse. In keeping with the culture of the day, boys and girls had their own door for entry. The building served as a school until 1925.

The school is now a part of 5-acre Sakonnet Farm, a family farm that sells seasonal produce and fresh eggs from free-range chickens. They also sell a variety of jams and jellies, and grass fed frozen beef. All of these items are sold on the honor system in a roadside building adjacent to the school.

The school exterior looks just like an 1800's one-room schoolhouse. The interior has been remodeled to include a modern gourmet kitchen, comfortable seating area, wood-burning fireplace and large screen TV. The master bedroom has a king bed and TV; the second bedroom has two bunk beds and a TV. The shared bath includes a whirlpool tub. The building has air conditioning and heat.

The school is a short walk from historic Tiverton Corners, which has a number of shops, restaurants, art galleries and ice cream stands. Guests also can roam around the farm, along with the chickens that own the place.

The Tiverton Four Corners School is open year round.

# Edisto River Treehouses

1 Livery Lane
St George, SC 29477
843-563-5051
www.canoesc.com
$$$$$

The Edisto River Treehouses offer guests the unique opportunity to spend the night in a tree house on a 160-acre private island on an unspoiled, undeveloped river. This is a rustic experience; there is no electricity, no running water and no indoor plumbing. It also requires moderate exertion paddling a canoe downstream. This stay was one of our favorite experiences of our trip.

The adventure begins at Carolina Heritage Outfitters on Highway 15 in Canadys (address above is GPS to get there.) We arrived at 9:30 and parked our car in their lot. After an orientation, we loaded our cooler and personal gear into their van. The van took us about 25 miles upstream to a launch area, where we put our canoe in and loaded our gear aboard. After a short, well-done, primer on canoe handling, we were off and on our own.

The canoe trip down the river was beautiful. The river is mostly pristine wilderness. The river is winding and thick vegetation lines the banks. The one- to two-mile per hour current did most of the work, but we did have to maneuver around the bends and fallen trees. We pulled up to sandy beaches every 45 minutes or so for a break from paddling and to stretch our legs. After four hours and 13 miles, we arrived at the tree houses.

Three tree houses are on the private preserve. Each one is tucked into the trees next to the river and has complete privacy. We stayed in the two-person tree house, but as the only guests that night, walked through the four-person and the six-person tree houses to see them. Each tree house is sturdily built, clean, well screened and comfortable. The tree house we stayed in has a deck with a picnic table and propane BBQ grill (propane provided). The house has a table and two chairs, a two-burner propane stovetop, cooking utensils and dishes, a futon, and a sleeping loft with a mattress and pillows. The nearby outhouse was clean (TP provided).

Mosquitoes were abundant as we walked about the preserve. We found that they were not a problem either out in the river or in the tree house. Mosquitoes tend to hover near the ground, and didn't bother us on the open-air deck. The deck also had citronella torches at the four corners, which kept them away in the evening, as well.

This experience required the most logistical planning of any of our stays. Our cooler was packed with food and beverages for a lunch on the river, dinner and breakfast at the tree house, and lunch again the next day paddling out. We also brought in sleeping bags, pillowcases, towels, toiletries, bug spray, and a clothing change, all in waterproof bags in case of tipping the canoe. (We didn't.)

Although the tree house had lanterns, we turned in shortly after dark, pleasantly exhausted from our trip. We slept comfortably in the well-ventilated loft with the sound of the river lulling us to sleep. In the morning, awakening birds served as our alarm clock. After our breakfast, we reloaded the canoe and continued downstream another ten miles, arriving back at Carolina Heritage Outfitters and our car by early afternoon.

The Edisto River Treehouses are open from March 1 to December 31 each year.

# Wildwater Chatooga

1251 Academy Road
Long Creek, SC 29658
866-319-8870
www.wildwaterrafting.com
$

Wildwater Chatooga has five yurts for group stays that accommodate up to 34 guests. The same company that operates Falling Waters Adventure Resorts in North Carolina operates Wildwater Chatooga. See page 198.

Thornewood Castle, WA

Nomad Ridge yurts, OH

# The Chattanooga Choo Choo Hotel

1400 Market Street
Chattanooga, TN 73402
423-266-5011
www.choochoo.com
$$ - $$$

The first Chattanooga Choo Choo ran from Cincinnati to Chattanooga in March 1880, and it will always be remembered because of the Glenn Miller song of 1941 that made it famous. In 1909, Chattanooga's Gateway Terminal opened and served train passengers for 51 years before closing in 1960. Today, the terminal is part of a hotel complex that includes three hotels, three pools, half a dozen restaurants, a bar, gift shop, and Victorian gardens. The hotel also includes 48 Victorian train car rooms.

The train car rooms are in remodeled passenger cars, with only two rooms to a car. Half a rail car is a big room! Our room contained a queen bed, flat screen TV, a couch/day bed, antique desk and chair, a private bath with tub and shower, and had wireless Internet available. The paneled walls were freshly painted, the room was decorated in a Victorian style, and it was very comfortable.

The terminal building is worth spending some time in. There are a number of displays of old memorabilia from railroads, and there is a magnificent, high-ceilinged, dark wood paneled bar to lounge in. But the most striking feature is the terminal dome. The dome is 75 feet in diameter and when it was built in 1909, it was the largest freestanding dome in the world.

While there are lots of restaurants at the hotel and nearby in downtown Chattanooga, you can keep the railroad theme going by having a pizza in the silver Dining Car on the rail just outside the lobby. You can stop before or after dinner on the adjacent rail to climb aboard one of the old, steam-powered Chattanooga Choo Choo's engines. The hotel is open year-round.

# The Antlers

1001 King Street
Kingsland, TX 78639
325-388-4411   800-383-0007
www.theantlers.com
Barbara & Dennis Thomas, Owners
$$$

In 1877, Martin King purchased land to the northwest of present day Austin where the Colorado and Llanos rivers meet, and founded Kingsland. In 1892, the Austin & Northwest Railroad built a bridge over the Colorado and a depot in Kingsland. This was the era of railroads operating resort destinations to boost ridership. So in 1900, the railroad began construction of a hotel in Kingsland.

The Antlers Hotel opened in May of 1901. It had 11 rooms and could accommodate extra guests on hammocks on the porches. There were gas lamps in every room, but no electric as the railroad thought electricity was a passing fancy. The hotel served as a getaway for Austin residents on weekends, and a hotel for travelling salesmen during the week. As the automobile replaced the railroad for vacationers, The Antlers declined and closed in 1923.

For 70 years, The Antlers was a private family retreat. In 1993, a couple from Austin purchased The Antlers and began restoration. The Antlers reopened in September of 1996. In addition to rooms in the historic hotel and several cabins on the 18-acre property on Lake LBJ, three cabooses and an 1880's era passenger coach named in honor of President McKinley provide lodging.

The cabooses all came from the Norfolk and Western line. Two of them have one double bed and two bunk beds. One caboose has just the double bed. All three have cupolas, a small kitchenette, baths and showers, heating and air-conditioning. The McKinley coach offers a spacious abode for four people and has one full and one half bath. All are clean and well kept up.

The Antlers has substantial frontage on Lake LBJ. It has four docks on the lake, three for boats and one for swimming. Canoes and rowboats are available to guests. Directly across the tracks from the hotel is The Grand Central Café, so you don't even have to leave the property for dinner.

We received a warm welcome at The Antlers. After we got settled into our caboose, we enjoyed a nice tour of the historic hotel and had a chance to see a number of artifacts and old photos from the 1900's. The Antlers is children-friendly and open year-round.

# El Cosmico

802 S. Highland Avenue
Marfa, TX 79843
432-729-1950
www.elcosmico.com
$$ - $$$


El Cosmico is an 18-acre nomadic hotel and camping property located in the high dessert on the west side of Marfa. Open since 2006, its credo is to live with minimal impact on the land. El Cosmico offers several lodging choices. We came here to experience their vintage travel trailers.

El Cosmico has restored eight travel trailers of various makes and sizes. We stayed in a Spartan Imperial Mansion from the 1950's. It had a comfortable bed, small kitchen, a seating/dining area and a bath with shower. The trailer was air-conditioned and a wood porch created an outdoor seating area for additional room. Guests park their cars at the lobby and walk into the property. Luggage carts are available if needed.

El Cosmico has tent-like abodes for rent, as well. They have eight canvas cabins. These cabins are 120 square feet. They have wood floors and come with a queen bed and chair. There are five smaller scout tents, accommodating two people. And there are three Sioux-style tepees, each 22-feet in diameter. The tepees have brick floors and are furnished with a queen bed, a day bed, and a love seat. Walk-on camping sites are also available. All of the tent-like abodes share a central bathhouse with showers, a tub, toilets and sinks. Towels and linens are provided.

Other El Cosmico amenities include the lobby, which sells beer, wine and snacks, an indoor and outdoor lounge, a hammock grove, an outdoor kitchen and dining area, bike rentals and wood-fired hot tub rentals on Friday and Saturday nights. There are several restaurants available in Marfa.

Just east of Marfa, an observation deck is located in an area where the mysterious Marfa Lights are frequently seen. The first written report of these lights was made in the 1950's, but they have reportedly been seen since the late 1800's. The lights appear to be small orbs of various colors, floating five or six feet over the ground at an indeterminate distance. Various explanations for the lights exist. Maybe you can solve the puzzle.

El Cosmico, offering a chance at adventure while chilling-out and doing nothing, is open year round.

# Old Schoolhouse
# Bed and Breakfast

401 Front Street
P. O. Box 1221
Fort Davis, TX 79734
432-426-2050
www.schoolhousebnb.com
$ - $$

The Old Schoolhouse B & B is nestled in a quiet pecan grove at the foot of Sleeping Lion Mountain. The building was built in 1904 and served actively as a school into the 1930's. The building has been remodeled several times, including the installation of modern electrical wiring and plumbing, but it still retains its original 22-inch thick adobe walls.

The schoolhouse has two guest rooms. The Reading Room is the larger bedroom. It is furnished with a king bed, and a sitting area with a sleeper sofa. The room has its own private entrance, as well as an entrance from the breakfast room. There is a porch off the private entrance and the room has a private bath.

The R & R Suite consists of two rooms. The 'Riting Room is a smaller bedroom with a queen bed. The 'Rithmetic Room is a private sitting room with a loveseat and a wingback chair. The suite has its own private bath.

A full breakfast is served to guests in the Breakfast Room each morning. During your stay, you have access to a guest refrigerator stocked with complimentary sodas and bottled water, a microwave, an icemaker, and a variety of teas and coffee. The Breakfast Room can also be used as a game room. The schoolhouse has heating and is cooled by an evaporative cooler.

The Old Schoolhouse Bed and Breakfast is open year round.

# Rainbow Hearth Sanctuary and Retreat Center

1330 Waterway Lane
Burnet, TX 78611
512-756-7878
www.rainbowhearth.com
Mariah Wentworth
$$ - $$$

Rainbow Hearth Sanctuary is located about an hour and a half northwest of Austin on the northeast shore of Lake Buchanan. Near the end of a long private road, it sits on a steep hillside and looks south with a commanding view of the lake.

A beautiful yurt is located in the trees above the main lodge. It has a large deck and a stunning attached bathhouse with a rainfall shower and two-person tub. The yurt is air-conditioned and is furnished with a king bed and two futon couches. Four suites are also available, two in the main lodge and two separate. Three have one bedroom and one has two bedrooms. All of the rooms have a private sitting room and a private bath. A hot tub with glass walls looking out to the lake is available by reservation in a separate building.

Rainbow Hearth is in an isolated location, far from restaurants. Breakfast is included with your stay, and lunch and dinner are available upon request. We enjoyed two organic meals during our stay that were both healthy and flavorful.

One of the major draws to Rainbow Hearth is the healing massage given by proprietor Mariah Wentworth. She is acknowledged to be a gifted healer and many guests report that her massage technique is the best they have experienced. Susan tried the massage and thought it outstanding. Sessions last from 90 to 120 minutes and focus not just on muscle relaxation, but also on whole body healing. Susan had been dealing with a tennis elbow all summer. Mariah traced the problem to a neck muscle. The day after the massage, her elbow was much better.

Rainbow Hearth has a beach house on the water where guests can sit and relax or pick up fishing poles to try their luck. After dinner we hiked up the hill above the lodge to Medicine Rock to watch a spectacular sunset. Rainbow Hearth Sanctuary is open year round.

# Tee Pee Motel & RV Park

4098 E. Highway 59 Business
Wharton, TX 77488
979-282-8474  (979-282-TIPI)
www.teepeemotel.net
$

The Tee Pee Motel is located about a mile outside of Wharton on what is now Highway 59 Business. George and Toppie Belcher built the motel in 1942 to serve travelers on Highway 60. It operated for 40 years, until the Interstate Highway rerouted traffic around Wharton. After sitting idle for 15 years, Barbara and Byron Woods bought the motel and restored it. It reopened in October of 2006 offering the restored tee pees and a new 50-pad RV park.

The motel has ten brown stucco tee pees for rent. They are a reminder of the golden age of American highway travel. They are clearly inspired by Frank Redford's Wigwam Villages, but were independent of his operation. Each tee pee is equipped with a full bed, private bath, couch, refrigerator, microwave, coffee maker and TV. All of the tee pees are air-conditioned. The remodeled tee pees are clean and bright.

Wharton is a small, quaint town. Several restaurants are within a few minutes drive of the motel. The Tee Pee Motel is, as they point out, one of only four such motels in the United States. It is open year round.

# Castle Creek Inn B & B

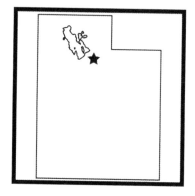

7391 S. Creek Road
Cottonwood Heights, UT 84093
800-571-2669    801-567-9437
www.castleutah.com
$$$ - $$$$

Lynn and Sallie Calder were looking for a unique place to open a bed and breakfast when they came across a partially built castle near Sandy, Utah. The castle was set in a grove of oak trees with a stream. The Castle Creek Inn provides a romantic lodging experience near all the attractions of Salt Lake City.

There are ten guest rooms at the Castle Creek Inn. Each room features a large, jetted tub, a fireplace, refrigerator, large screen TV with cable and DVD player, and free wireless Internet. In addition to the romantic interior, the landscaped grounds include shaded terraces, paths, waterfalls, streams and flowers.

Guests have the option of having a full breakfast in the grand dining hall or a Castle-lite breakfast in their room. The full breakfast includes fresh juices, baked goods and a hot entre. The Castle-lite breakfast includes juices, breads and yogurt.

The Castle Creek Inn is open year round.

# Castle Hill Resort and Spa

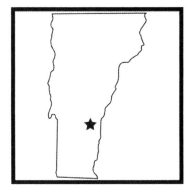

Routes 103 & 131
Proctorsville, VT 05149
855-785-4423   855-548-4696
www.castlehillresortvt.com
$$$$ - $$$$$

The Castle Hill Resort is located in southern Vermont a few miles east of Ludlow. The castle is an English Cotswold style mansion that was built by Allen Fletcher in 1905. In 1912, Allen Fletcher was elected Governor of the state. The castle is listed on the National Register of Historic Places and is a member of the Historic Hotels of America.

The elegant ground floor of the castle houses the library, dining rooms, kitchens and Governor Fletcher's private office. The woodwork and the fireplaces on the ground floor are original and are amazing in their intricacy. As an example, the pattern carved into the plaster ceiling of the library copies the pattern of the wallpaper in the stairway. The home was the first home in Vermont to have electricity, and the original Tiffany lights still work.

The ten guest rooms are on the second and third floors of the castle. The rooms feature hardwood floors, area rugs, and heirloom-quality linens, carved ceilings, period furniture and private baths. They are beautifully decorated and luxurious.

The Castle Hill Resort is open year round.

# Guilford Schoolhouse #10

Guilford, VT
802-257-0003
www.otterpondbindery.com
Susan Bonthron, Proprietor
$$$

Guilford Schoolhouse #10 is located in a very rural setting in southern Vermont. You may have noted above, there is no street address. Call Susan Bonthron for directions or find them on her website. Susan and her husband have restored and added to the schoolhouse to turn it into a charming place to stay.

Guilford was more heavily populated around 1800 than it is today. It was a "ten smoke" township. Schools were called "smokes" because they each had a fireplace that was tended by the children. School #10 was active from the late 1700's until around 1950, when a consolidated school was built.

The original schoolhouse has been restored and remodeled into a large living room and a bedroom. The living room is comfortably furnished with overstuffed chairs, a pullout couch, a dining table, and many antiques for decoration. The bedroom has a double bed, a room air-conditioner and a wood stove heater.

An addition to the schoolhouse contains a second bedroom, a full kitchen and a bath with tub, shower and a washer/dryer. The bedroom has a double bed and a door that opens onto a deck with a hot tub. Schoolhouse #10 is not a bed and breakfast, but Susan does provide the ingredients for guests to cook their own breakfast in the kitchen. She provided us with eggs, bacon, bread, butter, jam and coffee.

Guilford Schoolhouse is across the street from a former hippie commune of some renown from the 1960's and 70's. Ray Mungo has chronicled the adventures of the commune in the books "Famous Long Ago" and "Total Loss Farm".

Susan Bonthron also offers book art classes just walking distance down the lane from the schoolhouse at her Otter Pond Bindery. The Guilford Schoolhouse is open from April through mid-December.

# Moose Meadow Lodge

607 Crossett Hill
Waterbury, VT 05676
802-244-5378
www.moosemeadowlodge.com
Greg Trulson and Willie Docto, Owners
$$$$$

On June 16, 2013, Moose Meadow Lodge opened its two-story tree house as Vermont's premier "glamping" destination. This is a true tree house, suspended between two mature pine trees. It overlooks a trout pond and is built in a serene wooded setting. It is far enough away from the main lodge to feel private, yet only a short walk back to breakfast and the amenities of the lodge.

The first floor of the tree house holds a living room and a dining area. A deck wraps around the structure offering views of the woods and the trout pond. Also on the deck is a private outdoor shower, carved stone sink and an incinerating toilet. The second floor contains the bedroom furnished with a custom-made queen bed. The deck from the second floor offers more views of the pond.

Moose Meadow is comprised of 86 acres of wooded property and hills. A 30-minute hike up the marked trails is a glassed-in gazebo called the Skyloft, offering panoramic views from the highest point of the property. Moose Meadow is open year round.

# 1926 C & O Caboose

218 South Main Street
Lexington, VA 24450
540-463-2521
www.guestcaboose.com
Tom Bradshaw, Owner
$$$ - $$$$

Tom Bradshaw owns one of the most lovingly restored cabooses we encountered. He located it on a piece of bucolic, rolling farm country a few miles outside of Lexington near Natural Bridge, Virginia. (Address above is his office.) Staying here immerses you in railroad nostalgia, starting with a motion-detector turning on the railroad crossing flashers when you turn up the driveway.

Tom spent five years turning a caboose that was in bad condition into a beautiful restoration. The interior woodwork includes the original curved roof, red cedar walls and cherry floors. He installed a captain's double bed, custom built by Amish carpenters. The caboose is air-conditioned and heated. It is equipped with a day bed, a galley with a stove, a convection microwave and a small fridge.

There is a bath with shower, Bose sound system and satellite TV. The caboose is decorated with railroad memorabilia.

An extensive stone patio is outside and both a gas grill for cooking and a "hobo fire pit" for relaxing are available for guest use. The patio is lit by railroad lanterns and has comfortable seating.

The caboose will sleep two adults, or a small family. In addition to the day bed, two small children could sleep in the cupola with sleeping bags. The 1926 C & O Caboose is open from April through November.

# Prospect Hill Plantation

2887 Poindexter Road
Louisa County, VA 23093
540-967-0844
www.prospecthill.com
$$$ - $$$$$

In 1699, Roger Thompson homesteaded atop a hill in the foothills of the Blue Ridge Mountains, building a 10' by 10' cabin to live in. He married a widow with two sons a few years later and built a second cabin for himself and his wife, giving the boys the original cabin. By 1732, the family had 13 children and had built a Manor House. The homestead grew to a plantation, which at its peak was farming 1,500 acres of wheat and employed 20 slaves. During the Civil War, one of the slaves, Sanco Pansy, accompanied his master, William Overton, for four years of the war. They were with General Lee at Appomatax, and after Overton was pardoned and Pansy was set free, they walked home together, barefoot.

The Prospect Hill Plantation today encompasses 40 acres and offers the opportunity to stay in some of the original cabins. The cabins have been kept as close to their original function as feasible.

The cabins include the original 10' by 10' cabin, still called the "Boys' Cabin", Sanco Pansy's cabin, the cabin built for Roger Thompson and his wife, and several slave cabins.

The grounds around the house still have many of the trees that were planted around 1840. Of particular note are two magnolia trees of a rare variety, with elephantine leaves. The grounds include several ponds, a swimming pool that is open during the summer, a gazebo, and areas to walk.

We stayed in the "Boys' Cabin". Inside the original cabin, the walls were made of rough-hewn logs with the ax cuts visible. Two chairs were next to the hearth and we had a double bed. When we arrived, the side table held a tray of complimentary water, ice, soda, a half bottle of Pinot Noir and two chocolate chip cookies. A modern bath addition has been built onto the back of the cabin. This addition has a shower and Jacuzzi tub.

The plantation serves dinner on Friday and Saturday nights. From Sunday through Thursday, a dinner basket can be delivered to your cabin, with 24 hours notice. Breakfast is included with your stay and can be eaten at the Manor House or delivered to your cabin. It was a hearty breakfast with excellent bacon, a light soufflé, and a decadent homemade cinnamon roll. The Prospect Hill Plantation is open year round.

# Browns Point Lighthouse

Points Northeast Historical Society
1000 Town Center NE, Suite 180 PMB135
Browns Point, WA 98422
253-927-2536
www.pointsnortheast.net
$$

Browns Point marks the beginning of Commencement Bay and the entry into the Port of Tacoma. The first light on Browns Point was a lantern on a pole that was lit on December 12, 1887. A light keeper rowed out from Tacoma once a week to change the wick in the lantern and add oil. In 1903, the present lighthouse and keepers' cottage was built. The first keeper was Oscar Brown. He and his wife Annie occupied the cottage for 36 years.

The keeper's cottage sleeps six guests in three bedrooms. It is available for weekly stays, and makes for very reasonably priced accommodations while visiting the Tacoma area. The cottage sits inside a park that is open to the public, but a white picket fence separates the public area from the cottage. The cottage has a large porch facing the water for watching the marine activity. The beach is available for fishing, swimming and boating.

The grounds around the cottage are beautifully landscaped and maintained by a local floral society on a volunteer basis. The Coast Guard maintains the light and owns the park. The Points Northeast Historical Society maintains the keeper's cottage. The Browns Point lighthouse is open year round.

# Cedar Creek Treehouse

P. O. Box 204
Ashford, WA 98304
360-569-2991
www.cedarcreektreehouse.com
Bill Compher, Owner
$$$$$

Cedar Creek Treehouse is located near the Nisqually River Entrance to Mount Rainier National Park and overlooks Cedar Creek. The tree house is nestled 50 feet up a 200-year old Western Red Cedar. It has spectacular views to the south and east.

A picnic area is located at the base of the tree house and on the edge of Cedar Creek. The area has a picnic table, fire pit and charcoal grill. The creek provides the possibility of both trout fishing and swimming.

You enter the tree house by climbing several flights of substantial stairs. An enclosed observation deck is located about 40-feet above the ground. This area can be used for stargazing and bird watching. You remove your shoes here before ascending to the tree house.

The main room of the tree house has a futon couch, a small table with two chairs and a kitchen nook containing a gas stove, sink, icebox, cooking utensils and dishes. Complimentary coffee and tea are provided. Two smaller rooms are also at this level, a southern-facing sunroom with a day bed and a bathroom with a sink and a porta-potty. A ladder leads up from the main room to the sleeping loft. The tree house is off the grid, but small solar cells do power several 12-volt lights. The trunk of the cedar tree coming up through the floor and exiting out of the ceiling dominates the center of the room.

A tour of the Stairway to Heaven, Rainbow Bridge and Treehouse Observatory is included with your overnight stay. The Stairway to Heaven is a series of stairs encircling a large pine tree. Each step takes you up one foot and after circling the tree ten times you are 80-feet above the ground. The Rainbow Bridge is a suspension bridge to another tree that takes you up to the entry to the observatory, 95-feet up. When you reach the observatory level you are 100-feet above the ground and can enjoy a 360° view of Mount Rainier and its environs.

The Cedar Creek Treehouse opened in 1998 and has been recognized in numerous travel publications as one of the finest tree house rentals in the world. It is open from mid-May to mid-October each year. A two night minimum stay is required, but single nights are occasionally available between longer bookings.

# Cherry Wood
# Bed, Breakfast and Barn

3271 Roza Drive
Zillah, WA 98953
509-829-3500
www.cherrywoodbandb.com
Pepper Ferel, Owner
$$$$

The Cherry Wood B & B rests atop a hill in the rolling wine and fruit region of Washington's Yakima Valley. It consists of six tepees set inside an 80-acre working farm raising grapes, apples and rescued horses. In fact, all of the proceeds of the B & B go to the benefit of the rescue horses.

Each tepee is built on a cement and stone base and is furnished with a queen bed and a single day bed. The tepees have electricity, a small refrigerator, fans and lights, but no air-conditioning. Water comes from a well and is provided at a marble sink outside the tent. The cleanest port-a-potty we have ever seen was located nearby.

Two showers are located near the house inside a roofless wood structure.

Our tent had a BBQ grill and grilling utensils. You can use their wood to make coals, or you can bring your own charcoal. There were no dishes in the tent, but presumably those would be available upon request. In addition to the tepees, another private enclosure contained three soaking tubs that are available to guests. These "sunset tubs" rent by the hour and looked quite romantic.

The breakfast at Cherry Wood is one of our favorite breakfasts. Coffee is available at 7:00 and the breakfast is served on the patio of the house at 9:00. Ours consisted of juice, peaches in cream with basil, herb-baked eggs and toast. It was eaten in a beautiful setting, cooked perfectly and served by a friendly hostess.

While staying at Cherry Wood, we spent the afternoon visiting local vineyards, and there are a number of them nearby. You can take a guided tour of local vineyards on horseback for $225. The tour lasts from 11 to 4 and includes lunch. The Cherry Wood B & B is open year round.

# Evergreen Mountain Lookout

Skykomish Ranger Station
74920 NE Stevens Pass Hwy
Skykomish, WA 98288
360-677-2414
www.recreation.gov
$

The Evergreen Mountain Lookout is located about 20 miles north of Skykomish, Washington in the Mt Baker-Snoqualmie National Forest. Staying at the lookout tower is a rustic experience and requires a steep, scenic hike of 1.5 miles gaining 1,500 feet in elevation to 5,587 feet above sea level. The lookout was built in 1935 and is listed on the National Register of Historic Places.

The lookout is 14' by 14'. It is furnished with one twin bed and mattress and three additional mattresses. There is a table with four chairs, a propane stove, two propane lanterns, two cooking pots, a coffee pot and dishes. A vault toilet is located several hundred feet down the ridge from the lookout. There is no heat and no water.

Guests need to bring flashlights, sleeping bags, towels, dish soap, matches, a first aid kit, and garbage bags. Guests also need to bring all of their food and water for both cooking and washing. The lookout was closed when we visited this area, so we were unable to stay here. The ranger we spoke to advised us that it was prudent to bring in propane, cooking utensils and dishes, as well. She said that although these things are supposed to be provided, they occasionally wander off with prior guests. Bottom line – be self-sufficient.

The lookout is available to rent from late August through early October.

# Hobo Inn

54106 Mountain Highway East
Elbe, WA 98330
888-773-4637   360-569-2505
www.rrdiner.com
Elisa Fruzzetti, Conductor
$$

The Hobo Inn is located on the road to Mt Rainier National Park, about 14 miles from the park entrance. There are five cabooses for rent on the property adjacent to a dining car, named the Side Track Room. If you stop at the dining car for a drink, you can tell everyone that you got "Side Tracked".

The five cabooses sleep a maximum of four people each. They each have a queen bed, bath and shower. Several have cupolas with bunks in them, and several have jetted tubs. A stay at a caboose comes with breakfast in the dining car.

The dining car is a full service restaurant serving breakfast, lunch and dinner, and it has a full bar. The Hobo Inn is open year round.

Lakedale Resort canvas cabin, WA

Canvas cabin interior

# Lakedale Resort at Three Lakes

4313 Roche Harbor Road
Friday Harbor, WA 98250
800-617-2267   360-378-2350
www.lakedale.com
$$$

Lakedale Resort is located on scenic San Juan Island halfway between Roche Harbor and Friday Harbor. The resort encompasses 82 acres and has three spring-fed lakes that are stocked with fish. The resort offers a variety of lodging possibilities. You can stay in their ten room hotel, one of six log cabins, one of 14 canvas cabins, one 1978 Sovereign Airstream trailer, and many campsites.

We chose to experience Lakedale's "glamping" experience in a canvas cabin. The cabin is built on a wood deck and is furnished with a queen bed, a futon, a table with four chairs, sideboards, towels, a cooler and BBQ tools. Outside the tent are a fire pit with firewood and starter paper, four Adirondack chairs and a picnic table with an awning. Everything was clean and in good repair. The cabin is the glamorous part of glamping.

The camping part of glamping is the shared bath and showers. The bath facility was about a five-minute walk from our cabin. The showers are token-operated and you receive your tokens at check-in. We also had two porta-potties only a one-minute walk from our cabin for middle of the night use.

Breakfast is included with your stay and is served in a mess tent near the cabins. The breakfast was fruit, cereals, muffins or pancakes made in an automated pancake machine.

The resort offers many activities. You can fish the lakes and fishing gear is available for rent. You can also rent paddleboats and canoes. There is a swimming beach, as well. The general store sells camping and fishing supplies, some food, beer and wine, burgers and ice cream. There are many organized activities throughout the day for children.

One of the nicest surprises at Lakedale is their "Toasty Toes Turndown Service". In the early evening, an attendant came to our cabin and inserted two flannel-wrapped hot water bottles under the sheets at the foot of the bed. When we crawled in several hours later, those water bottles were heavenly in the chilly night.

Lakedale Resort is very child friendly. The resort is open from May 1st to September 30th each year.

# Lothlorien Woods Hide-A-Way

222 Staats Road
Snowden, WA 98672
503-281-9888
www.lothlorienwoods.com
$$

The Lothlorien Woods tree house is located about 20 miles north of White Salmon, Washington at the end of a two-mile logging road. It sits among pine trees on the edge of a working farm. You can see the keepers' house across a field. There are sheep on the farm and some may wander by.

The tree house is built on stilts and has three levels. At the ground level are a storage area and a table with chairs. A flight of stairs leads to an outdoor deck with a table and two chairs, a propane grill and a hot tub. The entry door leads inside to a small kitchen with a refrigerator/freezer, a stove and oven, sink and all your cooking utensils and dishes. Off the kitchen is a small living room area with a couch and a sound system (no TV).

A tight spiral staircase leads to the bedroom and bath on the top level. The bedroom has a queen bed and the bath has a shower. There is no air-conditioning, but at 2,000 feet elevation, the daytime temperature in July was in the 70's and it was 20 degrees cooler at night.

The tree house is very peaceful. There is no traffic noise. In fact, the hum of the motor on the hot tub is the only mechanical sound you will hear. Birds are abundant and you can occasionally hear animal sounds from the farm. Morning noises include wake-up calls from the roosters and dogs — you may want to bring earplugs if you are not an early riser.

Lothlorien is not a bed and breakfast. You will need to bring in your food for dinner and breakfast, or go for a very long ride back to White Salmon to find a restaurant. The tree house does have cooking basics like salt, pepper and garlic salt, but nothing else.

The Lothlorien Woods Hide-A-Way is open year round.

# Manresa Castle

651 Cleveland Street (P. O. Box 564)
Port Townsend, WA 98368
800-732-1281   360-385-5750
www.manresacastle.com
$$ - $$$


In 1892, prominent businessman Charles Eisenbeis and his wife Kate built a 30-room home that was known as the Eisenbeis Castle. The castle was the largest home in Port Townsend. Its walls were twelve inches thick, it had a slate roof and slate fireplaces and German craftsmen installed its custom woodwork. Charles died in 1902, and the castle stood empty for over twenty years.

In 1927, the Jesuits purchased the castle to use it as a training college. In 1928, the Jesuits added a large wing to the building. They also stuccoed the entire exterior to give the building a uniform look. They renamed the castle "Manresa Hall" after the name of the town in Spain where Ignatius Loyola founded the Jesuit order.

Since 1968, four successive owners have remodeled and restored the castle. Today the castle has 41 guest rooms on three floors, all with private baths. The rooms are decorated in a Victorian style and the hallways display many antiques. On the ground floor, a lounge with the original bar from San Francisco's Savoy Hotel is located in the castle's original drawing room. A restaurant occupies the original parlor and dining room.

A mezzanine floor was installed in what was the Jesuit Chapel. The Manresa Castle is a bed and breakfast, and breakfast is served in the lower level of the former chapel. The upper level of the chapel is a banquet space and the library is located in the former choir loft.

Manresa Castle has a couple of rooms that are supposedly haunted. Our room was not one of the haunted ones, and we didn't hear of any sightings at breakfast from any of the other guests. The Manresa Castle is open year round.

# New Dungeness
# Light Station Association

P. O. Box 1283
Sequim, WA 98382
360-683-6638
www.newdungenesslighthouse.com
$

The New Dungeness Lighthouse is located at the end of the five-mile long Dungeness Spit, which is reportedly the longest natural sand spit in North America. The Spit is reportedly one of the foggiest places in all of Puget Sound. The lighthouse was first lit on December 14, 1857 and has been in continuous operation since then. A separate keepers' house was built in 1904, and that house is available for guests.

Volunteer "keepers" can stay at the lighthouse for one week stays. The keepers' house has three bedrooms, two with queen beds and one with both a queen and twin bed. There are two full baths, and ample space for family living for up to seven people, including a recreation room with a pool table and a ping pong table. There are no roads to the lighthouse and it is a five and one half mile hike to get there. An off road vehicle transports you and your gear out to the lighthouse on a Friday or Saturday at low tide and picks up the prior week's keepers to return them ashore. The lighthouse is accessed from the Dungeness Recreation Area.

There are some duties associated with being a volunteer keeper at the lighthouse. You are required to watch a safety and orientation video before becoming a keeper. You can expect to be visited by day hikers from the recreation area during your stay, and you will be expected to provide them with tours of the lighthouse.

Children over the age of six are welcome at the lighthouse. You will need to bring all of your food for the week and do all of your own cooking. Water is provided from a 655-foot deep artesian well. The New Dungeness Lighthouse is open year round.

# Point No Point Lighthouse

9005 Point No Point Road
Hansville, WA 98340
415-362-7255
$$$$

There are several interesting stories about how the unusual name Point No Point was given to this lighthouse location. One story tells that US government surveyor Charles Wilkes named the point in 1841. He was looking for a location for a navigational light and hiked out onto a promising point. He was disappointed that the point wasn't more prominent, and hence the name.

The Point No Point Lighthouse is the oldest light on Puget Sound. It was first lit in 1879 and is situated within a 61-acre park with sandy beaches and hiking trails. Point No Point marks the transition from Admiralty Inlet to Puget Sound, which makes the point a great place to watch ships coming and going from Seattle, Tacoma and the naval base in Bremerton.

The vacation rental at the Point No Point Lighthouse is inside the historic Keeper's residence, and is a complete home that comfortably sleeps four guests. The house has two bedrooms upstairs with the master featuring a queen bed, and the second bedroom having two single beds. Also upstairs is a full bathroom and a small library. Downstairs, guests can enjoy a comfortable living room, a formal dining room with a breakfast nook, a full kitchen and a private yard. Every room has great views, and the front porch offers exceptional views of the waterway and Whidbey Island.

The Point No Point Light Station is also the national headquarters of the U.S. Lighthouse Society, a nonprofit dedicated to the preservation of America's lighthouses. Proceeds from the vacation rental are used to preserve the Point No Point Light Station specifically. The rental is open year round with a two-night minimum on weekends.

# Red Caboose Getaway Inn

24 Old Coyote Way
Sequim, WA 98382
360-683-7350
www.redcaboosegetaway.com
Charlotte & Olaf Leif, Stationmaster
$$$ - $$$$

The Red Caboose Getaway sits on the eastern edge of the city of Sequim, known as "The Lavender Capitol of America". The Getaway's stainless steel Zephyr dining car and a green caboose parallel the highway. Nine other cabooses are set in a roundhouse-like semi-circle to the back with a pond in the center of the circle.

Olaf has exercised his passion for trains by collecting cabooses that are each of a unique design. Charlotte has enhanced that by decorating each caboose to a theme. Six of the cabooses are available for lodging. Their names and themes are "Casey Jones", "Orient Express", "Circus", "Western", "The Lavender Limited", and "The Grape Escape".

All of the cabooses retain their original wood floors, original glass windows, pressure dials, railings and handholds. Most are equipped with a queen bed, a two-person whirlpool tub, toilet and sink, electric fireplace heater, flat screen TV with DVD and theme-appropriate movies, small fridge, and robes for your use.

We toured three cabooses and stayed in the "Orient Express". All of the themes were cleverly executed with great attention to detail. Our caboose had an interior stained glass window, golden mirror, movie posters and two authentic items from the actual Orient Express, an original room key and two cups with saucers for our morning coffee.

The Red Caboose Getaway is a B & B. Breakfast is served in the Silver Eagle, a 1937, stainless steel, art deco dining car. It is a four-course, gourmet breakfast. The menu varies daily, but it always consists of a fresh-baked loaf of bread, a savory dish, a sweet dish, and a small dessert. It was one of our favorite breakfasts.

The Red Caboose Getaway welcomes children age 12 and older. It is open from February through mid-December.

# Thornewood Castle

8601 N. Thorne Lane Southwest
Lakewood, WA 98498
253-584-4393
www.thornewoodcastle.com
$$$$$

Thornewood Castle is an authentic English Tudor Gothic castle whose history begins in England near the border with Wales in the 16th century. Chester Thorne, a wealthy Tacoma resident and one of the principal founders of the Port of Tacoma, had the castle taken apart and shipped in three ships to Washington in 1907. He reassembled the castle on the shore of American Lake as a summer home for his family.

The 27,000 square foot castle has 54 rooms, 22 bedrooms and 22 baths. The entry doors, the central staircase and many of the castle's wood panels are 500-year-old English oak. Over 100 of the windows are crystal that was manufactured in England and contain medieval stained glass pieces that date from 1300 to 1750. The castle contains an extensive collection of original artworks that date to 1700.

Upon entering the castle through the entry door, you are in the great room. A central stairway leads to the second and third floors. The formal ballroom is to your right and the Thorne family sitting room is to your left. The bedrooms are on the second and third floors and many have private bathrooms, while others have adjacent shared bathrooms.

The castle grounds today are on four acres. A sunken English garden sits on the north end of the property. The Olmstead Brothers, famous for designing Central Park in New York City, designed the garden. The grounds have extensive statuary on display.

Our breakfast was served in what was originally the ballroom on the first floor. It was extensive, including yogurt with granola, mixed fruit, Danish, toast, bacon and a baked egg dish.

Thornewood Castle has hosted two US presidents, Teddy Roosevelt and William Howard Taft. It has also appeared in three movies. The castle is open year round.

# Tree House Point

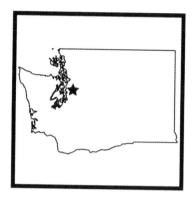

6922 Preston-Fall City Road, SE
Issaquah, WA 98027
www.treehousepoint.com
Pete and Judy Nelson
$$$$-$$$$$

While Tree House Point is located only 22 miles east of Seattle, and a mere two miles from Interstate 90, its serene setting in a forest beside the Raging River will seem much removed from the city's bustle. The bed and breakfast began in 2005 when Pete purchased the property and built the Temple of the Blue Moon, the first tree house on the site. Five additional tree houses, each uniquely designed and decorated, are now available for guest stay, as is a suite located in the main lodge.

Each of the tree houses is furnished with homemade queen beds, original artwork, and vintage pieces. Five of the tree houses are available for single or double occupancy, while Upper Pond can sleep four guests. The tree houses have electric service and heat and come with bed and bath linens. Several of the tree houses have a private toilet. All of the tree houses share common bathrooms on the ground with toilets, sinks and showers. The common baths supply soap, shampoo, body wash and hair dryers.

A continental breakfast is available from 8:30 until 10:00 each morning in the main lodge. It consists of fresh baked items, hard-boiled eggs or an egg based dish, homemade granola, yogurt, fruit, milk, tea and coffee. You should stop on your way to Tree House Point to pick up some prepared picnic style food to enjoy while staying there, as there is no food service, storage or prep sites on the premises. Several restaurants are located not too far away.

Tree House Point is open year round. From May through October, a two night minimum stay is required. Tree House Point hosts many weddings, so weekends are held for weddings until 60 days out. No children under 13 years of age are allowed, and the premises are non-smoking and pet free.

Pete Nelson is the founder of Nelson Tree House and Supply and is involved in preserving and building tree houses nationally.

# Don Q Inn

3658 Hwy 23 N
Dodgeville, WI 53533
800-666-7848   608-935-2321
www.donqinn.net
$ - $$$

Remember the old graffiti, "For a good time call ... ." Well, for a good time call the Don Q Inn, located in the rolling hills of southwestern Wisconsin. The fun starts from the highway as you approach the inn and discover a Boeing 377 Strato-Cruiser parked on the lawn. This plane was built for the military in 1952 and served carrying troops and equipment during the Korean War. Farah Fawcett signed the fuselage after shooting a commercial with the plane. The plane was purchased by the inn in 1977 and flown to the site. It is open for guests to tour.

The Don Q Inn has 25 fantasy rooms and suites decorated from naughty to nice available to guests, as well as some regular motel rooms. You can sleep in a recreation of a Gemini space capsule in Tranquility Base. Or sleep in the suspended gondola of a hot air balloon in Up, Up & Away. You can sleep in an igloo in Northern

Lights, or in a tented room in a 10-sided, 7-foot bed in Arabian Nights. The bed and chair in Mid-Evil comes with shackles. All of the accommodations are plush and most rooms are equipped with a hot tub. These tubs vary from heart shaped, hydrotherapy tubs to 300-gallon repurposed cheese vats, to whirlpools.

It is worthwhile to spend some time in the lobby area. A two-story tall circular fireplace dominates the lobby. The seating around the fireplace is on 17 barber chairs. There are two dentists' chairs in the lobby, as well. Your stay includes a complimentary breakfast, which is served in a small room off the lobby. Guests have access to the inn's indoor/outdoor pool.

Sam and Maddie's Restaurant is located adjacent to the inn. If you are staying on a cold or rainy night, you can get to and from the restaurant via an underground tunnel. The Don Q Inn is open year round.

# Old Schoolhouse B & B

2715 State Hwy 116
Waukau, WI 54927
920-685-7320
www.theoldschoolhouse.biz
Steve & Val Demuth
$

The Old Schoolhouse B & B is located in east-central Wisconsin in the small community of Waukau. The handsome brick building served as the Waukau Grade School beginning in 1926. The building has been remodeled to offer four guest rooms.

Each of the guest rooms is named for a former teacher at the school. The Mrs. Hemp room features a queen bed, a loveseat, a balcony and a private bath. The Mrs. Schoonover room has a queen bed and a shared bath. The Mrs. Wolfe room is decorated in an airplane theme in honor of the Experimental Aircraft Association, which holds its annual fly-in at nearby Oshkosh. The room has a queen bed and a shared bath. The Mr. Sticka room has two twin beds that can be converted into one king bad upon request, and a private bath.

The building has a common sitting room with a TV and DVD player. The common room has a fireplace, which is used during the cooler months. A library loft overlooks the common area.

The Old Schoolhouse is a bed and breakfast. The breakfast is a continental one available any time after 7:00 during the week with a full breakfast served at 9:00 on the weekends. The Old Schoolhouse is open year round.

# Spruce Mountain Fire Lookout Tower

Medicine Bow National Forest
Laramie, WY 82070
877-444-6777   307-745-2300
$

The Spruce Mountain Lookout Tower is located in south central Wyoming about seven miles west of the town of Albany on Forest Service Road 500. The 55-foot tall tower is located atop Spruce Mountain at an elevation of 10,003 feet, and has a panoramic view of the surrounding wilderness.

Staying at the lookout is a moderately rustic experience. You can drive your two-wheel drive vehicle to the tower and park adjacent to it. An outhouse is located near the base of the tower. There is also a picnic table and charcoal grill located on the tower grounds.

The tower itself is equipped with two twin beds with mattresses and accommodates up to four people. The tower cabin has a table, chairs, two-burner propane stove and oven, a propane refrigerator and propane lanterns. Cookware, dishes and cooking utensils are provided, as well. A bucket and pulley mechanism is available to lift your food and gear up to the tower level.

You need to bring all of your food and water for cooking and washing with you. You also need to bring sleeping bags or linens, towels, flashlights, garbage bags, and your own toiletries. Guests are expected to clean the tower and carry out their own garbage.

Reservations for the tower can be made six months in advance, and they stay fully booked. The tower is available from June through September.

# A Teton Treehouse

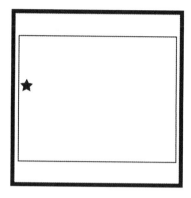

6175 Heck of a Hill Road
P. O. Box 550
Wilson, WY 83014
307-733-3233
www.atetontreehouse-jacksonhole.com
Chris & Denny Becker, Proprietors
$$$$ - $$$$$

A Teton Treehouse is not truly a tree house. It is a whimsical house in the trees that has been growing for over 40 years and has been a bed and breakfast for 28 years. It is set among tall pine trees and it feels like a tree house when you stay there. Your sense of elevation begins in the parking lot, reached after a steep drive up Heck of a Hill Road. The stairway to the house has a sign greeting you saying "Only 95 steps to go".

The tree house has six rooms for rent on four levels of the structure. Each room has a fine view of the Tetons and the Snake River Valley below. Each room has large windows, a private balcony and a private bath. When we arrived at 3:00 we found a sign inviting us to come in. We wandered around the common areas, which include a large living room with a two-story fireplace and loads of games to play, a loft dining area and a kitchen with complimentary beer, wine and soda available.

A Teton Treehouse offers an outstanding communal breakfast. Coffee was available earlier, but at 8:00, Denny rang the breakfast bell and all twelve guests gathered at the large table in the dining loft. Denny introduced all the guests and began serving stone-ground Irish oatmeal, home-made granola, cinnamon toast, lemon-poppy seed bread, juice, melon and coffee. Denny got the conversation among guests started and we all had a great time sharing travel tales. We didn't get up to leave for two hours.

A Teton Treehouse is located about ten minutes away from Jackson Hole, so there are numerous restaurants, saloons and galleries nearby to visit. The area is also the gateway to national parks, hiking trails, fishing and rafting on the Snake River. A Teton Treehouse is open year round.

Isle au Haut Lighthouse, ME

Caboose Motel, NY

Out N' About Treehouse, OR

Camp Ribbonwood safari tent, CA

The Original Treehouse Cottages, AR

Don Q Inn lobby, WI

Caribbean Motel, NJ

Jailer's Inn B & B cell room, KY

Middle Island Keepers Lodge, MI

Haceta Head Light Station, OR

# Also by Bruce & Susan Armstrong

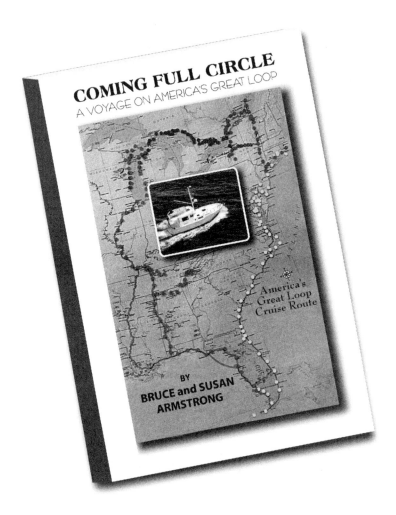

**Coming Full Circle: A Voyage on America's Great Loop**
is available at ArmstrongTravelVentures.com, Amazon.com
and GreatLoop.org.

**Coming Full Circle: A Voyage on America's Great Loop** tells the story of Bruce and Susan Armstrong's boating adventures. They spent four summers aboard their Nordhavn 35 *Gulf Cart* circumnavigating eastern North America, logging over 7,000 miles along the way. They survived two floods, weathered a tropical storm and outran a waterspout. Their route took them south from Naples around Florida's southern tip, then up the east coast, through Lake Champlain into Canada, across the Great Lakes, through Chicago and back to the Gulf of Mexico by way of America's inland rivers.

**Coming Full Circle** is a celebration of live-aboard boating and cruising and a commentary on the places they visited. It describes the joys and challenges of the journey with a sense of humor. It tells of hauling laundry through marinas, picking blueberries in Canada, hiking for groceries, watching gorgeous sunsets in isolated anchorages, and arriving at a new port in time for a local festival. It tells about the community of boaters on the Loop, of sharing long water crossings with other boats and celebrating with them at dinner that night. It is a story of discovery — new places, new friends, new foods and new ideas.

*"COMING FULL CIRCLE: A Voyage on America's Great Loop, makes for good reading, not only for the accounts of the trip's more harrowing moments, like the violent squall that hit them while returning from the Dry Tortugas to Key West, but also for the cruising advice you can glean from their descriptions of ports they stopped at along the way. Their writing is evocative enough to make you truly appreciate the appeal of this classic American cruise, even during the voyage's quieter moments."*
—Southern Boating Magazine